D1106752

Two Spanish Masterpieces

The *Book of Good Love* and *The Celestina*

Two Spanish Masterpieces

The *Book of Good Love* and *The Celestina*

María Rosa Lida de Malkiel

ILLINOIS STUDIES IN LANGUAGE AND LITERATURE: *Vol. 49*

THE UNIVERSITY OF ILLINOIS PRESS

URBANA, 1961

SECOND PRINTING, 1963

Board of Editors: HARRIS F. FLETCHER, JOHN R. FREY, AND PHILIP KOLB.

To

Y. M.

Accipe cui faueras paruum, Iacobe, libellum
"in quo censendum nil nisi dantis amor"

Acknowledgments

Collected in this book is the text of the six public lectures I delivered at the University of Illinois during my one-year tenure of a Miller Visiting Professorship (1959-60). I have tried to preserve as faithfully as possible the original wording, restoring only the paragraphs then omitted because of limitations of my time, and adding a minimum of footnotes.

It gives me sincere pleasure to reiterate here my gratitude to all those with whom this project has put me in debt: in the first place, the Department of Spanish and Italian, where I had the privilege to lecture and to teach throughout that year, and in particular its Head, Professor William H. Shoemaker, Professor and Mrs. Henry R. Kahane, and Professor Angelina R. Pietrangeli, whose thoughtfulness and generosity have been of invaluable help to me, and who have turned my stay *urbanissimae Vrbanae* into an unforgettable experience in friendship.

I am further very grateful to Professors Harris F. Fletcher, John R. Frey and especially to Professor Philip Kolb, as members of the Board of Editors of the *University of Illinois Studies in Language and Literature*, for their kind offer to recommend the publication of my lectures as a separate book. Thanks should likewise be given to Deans Frederick T. Wall and J. Austin Ranney, of the Research Board, who granted funds for the retyping of the text, and to Señora María Elena D. de Valdés who performed this task most conscientiously.

Finally, I would like to thank my Illinois students, as well as those of the Ohio State University, the University of Wisconsin, and the University of California at Los Angeles, to whom I have previously expounded some of the interpretations contained in the present book, and who have thus helped me to reappraise them critically, and to re-elaborate them with as much accuracy and lucidity as it was in my power to attain.

Contents

CHAPTER ONE

The Authors and Their Times

All students of the *Book of Good Love* and *The Celestina* agree that these are two masterpieces, but they disagree on virtually everything else. For this reason we should keep in mind something so obvious that it is likely to be forgotten: namely, that literary criticism — like all humanistic disciplines — cannot aspire to absolute truth, but rather to a relative and provisional truth within the limitations of the present state of knowledge. What I aspire to expound is not *the Truth;* it is *my* truth, or, to put it less rhetorically, it is the opinion which I have reached after spending many years carefully considering these two books and examining whatever I have been able to read about them.

The *Book of Good Love* and *The Celestina* are related to each other: the starting point of the plot of *The Celestina,* a drama in prose, is a certain Latin comedy of the twelfth century, *Pamphilus;* its free translation constitutes the longest and best known episode in the poem entitled the *Book of Good Love.* In elaborating this theme as a drama, *The Celestina* often does not follow the original Latin *Pamphilus,* but rather the intentional departures which characterize the free version in the *Book of Good Love.* These two masterpieces are typical examples of Spanish literature, not only because of their particular artistic fashion of representing reality, but also because both are intimately connected with European literature, and, at the same time, are in no less intimate contrast with it.

The *Book of Good Love* belongs to the first half of the fourteenth century; *The Celestina,* to the last years of the fifteenth and first of the sixteenth; each of these works is very representative of its period, and each of these periods is decisive in the cultural history of Spain. This is because in the Hispanic world medieval thought, art, and forms of life have exerted a deep and lasting influence, persisting as a foundation for more recent modes. In the Hispanic world, the Middle Ages are not just part of the distant past, and their immediacy is reflected materially, one might say, in the fact that the difference between medieval Spanish and the Spanish language of today is much less marked than that between medieval French and the French of today, and very much less so than that between medieval and present-day English. With an almost unconscious modernization of the sounds and none whatever in morphology, lexicon, and syntax, parts of the *Book of Good Love* and scenes from *The Celestina* are recited and performed today before the general, non-academic public of Spain and of Spanish America. The *Book of Good Love* and *The Celestina* are not historical relics, two antiques whose dates and contents one must memorize to pass college examinations: they are two living books.

Very little is known about the authors of these works. All that we know about the author of the *Book of Good Love* is what he declared in his poem, that is, his name and occupation: "I, Juan Ruiz, archpriest of Hita" (stanzas 19bc = 575a).[1] We also know the date of the two versions of his work: 1330 in one manuscript and 1343 in another, more recent and more extensive (1634ab). Facing such meager information, first the copyists and then the critics have attributed to the poet himself the various and delightful happenings which he recounts in the first person, just as medieval readers converted Pamphilus into the author of the comedy of which he is the protagonist; and, to give a more famous example, just as the common people of Ravenna saw in Dante the traveler who in life had gone through Hell, Purgatory, and Paradise. The biography thus compiled is quite entertaining and melodramatic: naturally, it is unreasonable to expect from it any correspondence with reality.[2]

[1] Throughout these lectures I refer to the edition of the *Book of Good Love* (*Libro de buen amor*) by J. Ducamin, Toulouse, 1901; and to the edition of *The Celestina* (*La Celestina*) by J. Cejador, 2 vols., Madrid, 1913. I quote the *Book of Good Love* by stanza and line; *The Celestina,* by act and page. The original spelling of "Rojas" was "Roxas."

[2] Thus, from stanza 493ab "I noticed over there in Rome, where sanctities abound / That every one to Money bowed and humbly kissed the ground" (Elisha K. Kane's translation, New York, 1933), earlier scholars inferred a visit to the papal court. Now, in Juan Ruiz's lifetime, the papal court resided at Avignon; besides, F. Lecoy, *Recherches sur le "Libro de buen amor,"* Paris, 1938, pp. 237 ff., has shown that the whole passage is based on twelfth- and thirteenth-century satire, in Latin, against Roman simony. What the lines quoted mean is not that Juan Ruiz actually visited Rome, but that he kept in close contact with goliardic thought and literature. For the supposed self-portrait in stanzas 1485 ff., see Kane, "The personal appearance of Juan Ruiz," *Modern Language Notes,* XLV (1930), 103-108. As regards the annotation at the end of the Salamanca MS stating that Juan Ruiz composed his poem while imprisoned by order of his Archbishop, see my paper "Nuevas notas para la interpretación del *Libro de buen amor,*" *Nueva Revista de Filología Hispánica,* XIII (1959), 69 ff. Concerning the danger of anachronistically reinterpreting medieval literature in biographical terms cf. D. Čiževsky, "On the question of genres in Old Russian Literature," *Harvard Slavic Studies,* II (1954), 105-115.

The situation of *The Celestina* is infinitely more enigmatic. The work commonly called *The Celestina,* because of the name of its most popular character, appeared first under the title *Comedy of Calisto and Melibea,* composed of sixteen acts, the first considerably longer than the others. When and where did it appear? No one knows for certain; however, starting from an array of conjectures, scholars believe that the copy in the Library of the Hispanic Society of New York, lacking the first and last pages, is one of the editio princeps, presumably published in Burgos, in 1499. But the first edition whose date and place are really known is that of Toledo, 1500, followed by that of Seville, 1501. These and subsequent editions fail to mention the name of the author but, at the end of the text, in stanzas added by the proofreader, we are told that the name and homeland of the author may be found in acrostic in some stanzas which precede the text. The acrostic spells out the following: "The Bachelor [that is: Bachelor in Law] Fernando de Rojas finished the Comedy of Calisto and Melibea and was born in Puebla de Montalbán." In the seventh stanza and succeeding ones, mediocre verses at that, as well as in a letter from "The author to a friend," written in excellent prose, Rojas declares that he had found the first act in Salamanca without the author's name and that, as a diversion from his professional duties, he had completed the work during a two-week vacation. In 1502 there appears in Seville and in Toledo a new version, with the title *Tragicomedy of Calisto and Melibea,* and in addition a prologue, in which the author justifies the adoption of the term *Tragicomedy* instead of *Comedy.* He also mentions the readers' reaction, the majority of whom desired "that I should enlarge myself in the pursuit of the delight of these lovers."[3] And, in fact, the editions of 1502 interpolate five more acts into the middle of Act XIV, and among them the most beautiful love scene of the drama — and of all Spanish literature. Moreover, these editions of 1502 retouch the preceding text, above all starting from Act II, by means of alterations, suppressions, and in particular, of additions, some rather long. Also retouched are the letter from "The author to a friend" and the verses in praise of Act I, which now propose as authors "Cota or Mena," two famous poets of

---

[3] James Mabbe's translation, *The Spanish Bawd represented in Celestina or the Tragicke-comedy of Calisto and Melibea,* London, 1631, edited by H. Warner Allen, London, 1908, p. 5. For a bibliographical inventory of *The Celestina,* see Clara Louisa Penney, *The Book called "Celestina" in the Library of the Hispanic Society of America,* New York, 1954. Add a Russian translation, Moscow, 1959 and G. J. Brault, "English translations of *The Celestina* in the sixteenth century," *Hispanic Review,* XXVIII (1960), 301-312.

the preceding generation. Therefore, the long first act is by an "older author," perhaps Rodrigo Cota or Juan de Mena; the fifteen remaining acts of the first editions and the twenty remaining acts of the editions from 1502 onward are by Fernando de Rojas. A careful examination of the text — sources, style, retouching, dramatic technique, presentation of the characters — shows, in fact, perceptible differences between Act I and the remainder. Furthermore, there are already signs of collaboration in the *Comedy,* but these are distinctly more marked in the *Tragicomedy.* The notion of collaboration clashes with our judgments on artistic creation and individuality, but it is well known that in fifteenth- and sixteenth-century painting the unity of authorship frequently refers to the workshop rather than to the individual painter. Literary collaboration is no less frequent, and T. S. Eliot has said: "In Elizabethan drama, the critic is rash who will assert boldly that any play is by a single hand."[4]

The Bachelor in Law Fernando de Rojas, then, is the principal author of *The Celestina.* As far as is known, he wrote no other book, and no contemporary or even near-contemporary author names him. So strange is it that the author of a work of such extraordinary merit and success as *The Celestina* should have left no trace that a renowned French Hispanist, scoffing at Spanish naïveté, went to the extreme of arguing that Fernando de Rojas was simply an imaginary name, a pseudonym. Two years later, a Spanish scholar discovered the record of a trial by the Inquisition of Toledo, 1525, in which the victim, one Álvaro de Montalbán, declares that he has a daughter named Leonor, "the wife of the Bachelor Rojas who composed *Melibea.* . . ." And when, in accordance with their hypocritical proceedings, the Inquisitors invited him to name a counsel for the defense, Álvaro appointed "Bachelor Fernando de Rojas, his son-in-law . . . who is a convert." The Inquisitors rejected Rojas, and told the accused to name "someone beyond suspicion." In the course of the trial, the curate of the town of Montalbán added that there was hardly a person in it who had not been "reconciled"; that is: in Rojas' birthplace (as in other small Spanish towns, Lucena or Carrión, for example), almost the entire population had been composed of Jews who had no choice but to become converts, and who continued to be as Jewish as before, for which reason the Inquisition had punished them; this is

[4] *Elizabethan Essays,* London, 1934, p. 119 (apropos of Cyril Tourneur). For a more detailed examination of *The Celestina*'s authorship, see the Introduction to my forthcoming book *La originalidad artística de "La Celestina,"* to appear in Buenos Aires.

the meaning of the euphemism "reconciled." Later, other documents came to light. In a long trial, a grandson of Fernando de Rojas succeeded in proving that he belonged to the lesser nobility (*hidalgos*). Some critics have maintained that, being a nobleman, Rojas could not have been a Jew. But the two facts were entirely independent; the father and the uncles of Saint Teresa were also involved in lawsuits to prove that they were part of the lesser nobility, and during the course of the inquiry it came to light that the father of the plaintiffs (Saint Teresa's grandfather) was a converted Jew who had been implicated in annoying difficulties with the Inquisition for continuing to practice Judaism. And the clearest example is of King Ferdinand the Catholic, who was himself of remote Jewish origin on the side of his mother, Doña Juana Enríquez, daughter of the Admiral of Castile.

Perhaps the most interesting of Rojas' documents is his will, containing an inventory of his possessions (including his Spanish books) and naming his sons, daughters and sons-in-law, also converted Jews, all of which shows that he remained very much attached to his lineage. Some critics object that whatever his origin Rojas' Christianity cannot be doubted, since he lived and died (1541) as a Christian, he ordered masses for the repose of his soul and was buried in a church, in the Franciscan habit. These critics (one from the United States, the other from Argentina), through their incapacity even to imagine the unbearable pressure which the Inquisition imposed, render the greatest homage to the liberty of our times and, above all, of our Americas. For, had Rojas refused to live as a Christian, he would have gone directly to the stake. If, at the time of his death, he and his family had failed to observe scrupulously all Christian rites, his family would have paid dearly. "Paid" is not a metaphor: it was enough that, on being presented the crucifix, the dying man should turn away his head, for the Inquisition to seize his inheritance and persecute his family. True, Fernando de Rojas, the convert who was not "beyond suspicion" in 1525, was buried in the Franciscan habit. But an old Spanish proverb says: "Judge not a man by his frock" [*debajo del sayal, hay ál*], and a famous case of the Inquisition in Mexico reveals that a certain convert (by the name of Antonio Machado) was buried in the church wearing the habit of an Augustinian friar. Years later, his daughter, caught by the Inquisition, confessed under torture that, out of obedience to her father's will, she had shrouded him according to Jewish custom, covering the shroud with the monk's habit. Only Heaven knows what was underneath the

Franciscan habit in which Fernando de Rojas was buried — and what he ensconced in the depths of his soul.[5]

This is all that we know concerning the biography of Juan Ruiz, Archpriest of Hita, author of the *Book of Good Love,* and of Bachelor Fernando de Rojas, principal author of *The Celestina.* Their books, however, remain as revealing documents, especially if we examine them in the light of their milieu. The era of Juan Ruiz is the first half of the fourteenth century, when local circumstances fostered the growth of an art which had less in common with the rest of Western Europe than in previous centuries — a distinctively Spanish art. Until the twelfth century, the war of reconquest against the Moors who had invaded Spain in 711 unified Castile's energies and simultaneously limited her cultural development; the learned men adopted as a model the Latin and French literature of Christian Europe beyond the Pyrenees. But in the early thirteenth century, the Reconquest progressed extraordinarily, with the result that from that time on Arab territory was confined to the kingdom of Granada. There still took place a few important battles but, in fact, the conflict was resolved: the Arabic menace had been dispelled. One consequence of this change was the lack of political unity and the rise of feudalism. Great lords, enriched during the Reconquest, seized power during the disastrous reign of Alfonso the Learned and during the restless times of his successors. Another consequence was that, with the progress of the Reconquest, a considerable number of the non-Christian population was incorporated into the realm. For the moment they were permitted freedom to practice their faith and customs, not because of a true sense of religious tolerance, but because they were needed to continue plying their trades, of which the Christian warriors were ignorant and disdainful. Moreover, the reconquest of the great Andalusian cities caused Spain to turn to their civilization, depending less exclusively

[5] See *La originalidad artística de "La Celestina,"* Introduction, n. 11, and the literature there quoted; add R. F. Giusti, "Fernando de Rojas, su obra de humanidad española y de arte renacentista," *Boletín de la Academia Argentina de Letras,* XII (1943), 128, and O. H. Green, "Fernando de Rojas, *converso* and *hidalgo,*" *Hispanic Review,* XV (1947), 384-387. Concerning Antonio Machado, see A. Toro, *La familia Carvajal,* Mexico City, 1944, vol. I, 157 ff. If, as so many of his townsmen, Rojas (or his family) had been "reconciled" and the sanbenito was hanging in the principal church, as was customary, the desire to escape from this note of infamy would provide a more cogent cause for his departure from Puebla de Montalbán than the difficult temper of Puebla's lord, the reason advanced in the trial; compare the case of the great Fray Luis de León's parents, who left the town of Belmonte, in whose collegiate church the sanbenitos of two ancestors had been exhibited (A. Coster, "Luis de León," *Revue Hispanique,* LIII [1921], 47).

on the Latin and French tutelage common to the rest of Europe. The interpenetration between the two cultures was at no time greater: Juan Ruiz understands and quotes phrases in colloquial Arabic, and the fact that he quotes them without translating means that they were also currently understood by his public. In the thirteenth century, many Arabic scientific treatises and some literary works of didactic intent had been translated; the great authors of the fourteenth century did not translate: they artistically elaborated motifs from that literature, adopting its structure and its didactic basis. A great interpreter of Spanish culture, Don Américo Castro, has rightly spoken of the *mudejarismo* of Juan Ruiz.[6] *Mudéjar*, that is, 'reserved,' is the term used for Arabs who continued to practice their religion in a Christian community. These Arabs were in the main able artisans who developed a particular style, a fusion of Arabic and Gothic. It represents the first national style of Spain. And the *Book of Good Love,* also a fusion of elements common to the literature of Christian Europe and to the Semitic literatures of Spain, constitutes a work of *mudéjar* art, more national than the great works of previous centuries.

The *Book of Good Love* says much about its author; it reveals a poet fascinated by concrete reality. Everything in the book is immediate, direct, and sensuous. All happenings have a precise date; their locale is this or that Spanish town or village; all abstract personifications — the plague of medieval didacticism — turn into living people. The poem abounds in brief and graphic descriptions, it is very rich in images and, for the first time in Spain, it recreates popular speech with inimitable charm. There is, moreover, a good deal of movement and traveling; all Spain figures in it, from Biscay to Andalusia. Not only the cities, but also the rough *sierras,* the fields, and the tillers in the fields, are pictured with rare detail and attention.[7] For Juan Ruiz, like for many a medieval author, reading is not an activity apart from and opposed to living experience; on the contrary it is one of its

---

[6] *España en su historia: cristianos, moros y judíos,* Buenos Aires, 1948, p. 445; cf. the second, considerably modified edition of this work, *La realidad histórica de España,* Mexico City, 1954, p. 413, and the English translation by E. L. King, *The Structure of Spanish History,* Princeton, 1954, p. 403.

[7] On the other hand, the silence about the calamities of his own time is highly symptomatic of Juan Ruiz's optimistic temper. From his poem we would never guess that the young king Alfonso XI was actively striving to subdue the unruly nobility, that he was engaged in a long campaign against the *benimerines* Moors (a campaign in which he was effectively assisted by Juan Ruiz's Archbishop, Don Gil de Albornoz), and that Black Death, which was soon to kill the Castilian King, was ravaging Europe. Only stanzas 326d and 1696 f. seem to harbor allusions to Alfonso XI's monetary reforms, and to his concubinage with Leonor de Guzmán.

highest forms. For this reason he delights in exhibiting his reading; he enjoys quoting the Bible, the best-known texts of canonic and civil law, various moral treatises, Ovid's *Art of Love,* the comedy of *Pamphilus,* Esopic fables,[8] and, without expressly referring to it, he reflects the magnificent satirical poetry of the so-called "goliards." The prestige of Latin was such that medieval authors preferred not to name their vernacular sources, but the *Book* contains several narrative and lyrical episodes of probable French descent. An example of this is the ribald tale of Pitas Payas (474 ff.), a true *fabliau* in its theme, structure, and licentious tone, whose characters are French and babble a combination of Spanish and French or Provençal in such a way that, recited by a good minstrel — and let us not forget that the *Book of Good Love* is composed to be spread through the recitation of minstrels rather than through individual reading — it would make a Castilian audience burst with laughter. Of course, Juan Ruiz must have lent an attentive ear to the literature of his own land; traces of the production of the previous century and allusions to the fashion of his own days are visible in his poem. Folk songs must also have appealed to him: the echo of one, the nun's complaint, appears in the most passionate scene of a long episode (1499 ff.); and he was clearly familiar with the fine letters of non-Christian Spain.

Starting with its title, the poem displays the medieval piety of its author, since "good love" is, on its highest plane, love of God; on a lower — but still worthy — plane it is courtly love, that is, worldly love. The piety of this fourteenth-century poet has nothing of the calculating and somber fanaticism of Philip II or of the prim piety of more recent times. Juan Ruiz is very little given to abstract theology and morality; he hates and fears as personal enemies the Devil and above all Death — with a profound horror which is the reverse of his love of life. With the absolute confidence of the vassal in his feudal lord, he confides in the Virgin, his personal and immediate protector, his intercessor before Christ. God the Father, abstract and remote, appears in the solemn invocation at the beginning of the *Book,* and almost never again. With great frequency, Juan Ruiz speaks of prayers, ceremonies, vows, festivities, what one eats and is forbidden to eat during Lent; he never refers to intimate piety or meditation.

---

[8] A meaningful contrast is provided by Benito Pérez Galdós's historical novel, *Carlos VI en la Rápita* (1905), whose best fictional character is the Archpriest of Uldecona. This modern reincarnation of Juan Ruiz proclaims emphatically his contempt for books and learning: "My child, I have no library and I don't feel the slightest need for one. I never open a book. . . . My library . . . is Mankind. . . ." (Chap. XIX).

His is an absolutely orthodox devotion, very respectful of the organization of the Church and quite indulgent towards the moral weaknesses of the ecclesiastics. Thus, the poet jokes tirelessly about the avarice, gluttony, and frailty of nuns, friars and archpriests, but he speaks very seriously of the grievous sin which a confessor commits when he absolves a church member who does not belong to his parish. As he is so sure of his faith, Juan Ruiz can afford to engage in familiarities which scandalize less secure readers; a suitor says to his lady when proposing to her (661c): "I love you more than I love God," which sounds perfectly inoffensive in Spanish, because God is, simply, the highest term of comparison and even today it is perfectly natural to say in Spanish, "so and so is kindlier than God," and even, "so and so is more wicked than God," which only means "so and so is utterly wicked."

Another aspect of Juan Ruiz's serene and unruffled faith is his delight in the parodying of devout texts. It is well known that religious parody in no sense implies criticism, rebellion, or scorn of the rites or words parodied; central to it is a joy of relaxation, the game of applying phrases or ceremonies, normally regarded with the greatest reverence, to things which are very distant or totally opposed in value. This is why Chaucer in *The Legende of Good Women* applies devout formulas, taken from saints' lives, to the heroines of Greco-Roman love stories (*Incipit legenda Cleopatrie martiris, Egipti regine; Explicit legenda Cleopatre martyris,* etc.); and why to the ecclesiastic John Skelton, steeped in liturgy, it must have seemed extremely amusing to celebrate the death of a child's sparrow in conformity with the Roman Office for the Dead and interpolating the original Latin verses. For this very reason, and to the great astonishment of the foreign reader, the devout Hispanic literature is one of the richest in this class of parody from the twelfth century to the present time, and Juan Ruiz is the most assiduous, the most jovial, the most audacious of these parodists. Religious parody is a stylistic device permeating the entire poem. Let one example suffice: on lamenting the death of the go-between (who answers to the expressive name of *Trotaconventos,* 'Dame Convent-trotter'), Juan Ruiz parodies an epistle (LX, *Epitaphium Nepotiani*) in which Saint Jerome laments the death of a young priest. As Saint Jerome affirms that the young priest is in Paradise, "with Christ, and united in the saintly choir," so Juan Ruiz assures the go-between (1570abc):

> Indeed, you are in Paradise, among the martyrs' crew
> Because on earth you suffered martyrdom for lovers two.

The *Book of Good Love* also discloses a good deal about Juan Ruiz's relationship to the non-Christian minorities comprised in the Castilian population around the middle of the fourteenth century. The expanded edition of 1343 begins with a solemn prayer whose first verses are:

> Thou, Lord God, who ledst from Egypt, out of Pharaoh's power
> The Jews, that accursed nation . . .

But this solemn approach is merely the façade; within the *Book* its author shows cordial familiarity with the Jewish community. After all, the one in Hita was important, and in Toledo, where he in all likelihood pursued his studies, resided the most prosperous and most cultured Jewish population of Europe. Juan Ruiz was familiar with their holidays, their businesses, their foods, their prayers. To emphasize the fact that a certain lady is jealously guarded by her relatives, he says with complete spontaneity (78d): "They kept my lady stricter than the Jews their Torah keep." Concerning his lyrical output, we read this surprising declaration (1513ab):

> Next after that I wrote the words to many a dancing song,
> For Jewesses and Mooresses, and all that merry throng.

Though, unfortunately, these songs have not come down to us, it may be affirmed that if Juan Ruiz composed much for Jewish and Moorish singing and dancing girls, he also learned much from their repertoire, as his *Book* shows. The declaration cited continues thus:

> I also wrote some ditties for blind men without sight,
> Others for student roisterers who gad about at night,
> Others to sing from door to door for many a beggared wight:
> Ten folios full of mocking songs and ballads full of spite.[9]

Council after council of ecclesiastic authorities warned the clerics to steer clear of scurrilous amusements, to keep aloof from vagrant clergymen and, of course, not to befriend infidels. Conceivably Juan Ruiz exaggerates his bad conduct here, to show himself as the epitome of the sinful clergyman, just as Chaucer satirically underlines the weaknesses of the worldly nuns in the delightful portrait of Madame Eglantine, the prioress. But if Juan Ruiz exaggerates, he does not entirely invent, since some of his songs for mendicant students and for blind men (a lyrical genre practiced among the Arabs) have been preserved. The remaining portion of this personal confession enumerates the musical instruments unsuitable for the accompaniment of Arabic songs. He twice quotes Arabic songs (1229b, 1516c), both times in the original language. Beyond any doubt, Juan Ruiz knew

[9] Some expressions in this stanza are borrowed from Kane's translation.

intimately the poetry and music of the *mudéjares*. But not only the poetry and music. The above mentioned confession comes after a brief and exquisite episode in which a young Moorish girl rejects the poet's love. In a word: Juan Ruiz is a *mudéjar* artist, in whom the joy of Castile, with her three religions, flowers as never before nor since.

The climate surrounding Fernando de Rojas, at the end of the fifteenth and the beginning of the sixteenth centuries, is very different. In the first three quarters of the fifteenth century, the end of the Reconquest appeared so near that the war passed to a secondary level. Castile just began to break out of the isolation to which her "holy war" had reduced her, and Aragon, which had extended its domination to Naples and Sicily, brought to Spain the influence of the Italian Renaissance. Castile, no longer held together by the Arab danger, split into a very weak royal power and a turbulent nobility which were locked in almost ceaseless civil strife, while the people suffered the economic vacuum caused by the end of the Reconquest: on the one side, it was no longer possible to gain rapidly fortune and honors with arms in hand; on the other, the people discovered that they neither knew nor cared to learn how to work, to go into business, or to act as administrators; moreover they grew aware of the fact that those who exercised these activities were Moors and, above all, Jews. From this shock derives the growing rancor against the Jews, not among the nobility or high clergy, but among the humbler classes and the low clergy; a hostility which breaks out into mob violence as of the end of the fourteenth century. The princes in turn begin to realize that the *pogrom* is an effective means of distracting and rewarding a population, exasperated by misery and insecurity. By way of self-defense, many Jews espouse the State religion. Then, protected by baptism, they abandon the defenseless ghetto and are in a better position than ever to stand out in society. It is sufficient to remember Salomón Haleví, Rabbi of Burgos, who after his conversion became Bishop of Burgos, Chancellor of Castile and guardian of the young King John the Second; his son, Alfonso, succeeded him as Bishop of Burgos and represented the Spanish clergy in the Council of Bâle. The convert Luis de Santángel was the person who swayed the Queen in favor of Columbus and who advanced from his private purse the sum necessary for equipping the three caravels. Needless to say, the success of these converts excites more than ever the rancor of the humbler-class "old Christians."

In 1479 Ferdinand of Aragon and Isabella of Castile united the kingdoms of Spain; Isabella did so after five years of fighting against the legitimate heiress to the throne. With much luck, few scruples, and sufficient astuteness to resolve the immediate problems — remember that Machiavelli in his treatise *The Prince* took Ferdinand as a model — the Catholic Sovereigns succeeded in suppressing the feudal nobility and transforming it into a palace nobility. They further managed to reconquer Granada, a feat which, to say the truth, no longer had any great military or political value but had an enormous emotional value, infinitely greater, for the contemporaries, than the discovery of America that same year. Following the example of their predecessors, Ferdinand and Isabella rewarded the populace with repressive measures against the Jews. They did this in 1483 with the establishment of the Inquisition, destined above all to harass the converts, and also in 1492, with the expulsion of the Jews from all of Spain, after preparing public opinion through a sensational trumped-up murder trial.[10]

None of these converts has left a diary or memoirs. But it is not too bold to conjecture that their lives must have been a continual nightmare of fear, shame, and remorse, a perpetual conflict between two traditions.[11] Only once does Fernando de Rojas lift the dramatist's mask to pour out the personal bitterness of a convert persecuted by the Inquisition. You will find this passage in Act VII; Celestina men-

[10] The trial of the Holy Child of la Guardia, whose death was imputed to several Jews and converts; see the documents published by P. Fidel Fita, *El Santo Niño de la Guardia* (*Estudios históricos*, vol. VII), Madrid, 1887 (also in *Boletín de la Real Academia de la Historia*, XI, 1887, 7-160), and the discussions by I. Loeb, "Le Saint enfant de la Guardia," *Revue des Études Juives*, XV (1887), 203-232, and by H. C. Lea, "El Santo Niño de la Guardia," *English Historical Review*, IV (1889), 229-250; Lea points out "the fortunate coincidence of such affairs with measures in preparation against Jews" (pp. 230, 231, 235, and especially 244). The duplicity of the Catholic Sovereigns in this matter is proven by their guarantee to extend to the native Jews of Granada the same privileges as were accorded to the *mudéjares* at the surrender of the city (November 25, 1491), that is, barely four months before signing the decree of expulsion. No less demonstrable is the fact that the religious feelings of Ferdinand and Isabella had little to do with the expulsion: a short time before, Isabella had no scruple in accepting rich presents from the Jewries (see J. Amador de los Ríos, *Historia social, política y religiosa de los judíos de España y Portugal*, Buenos Aires, 1943, vol. II, 202), and both availed themselves up to the last moment of the services of Isaac Abravanel and Abraham Senior. Similarly, when in 1502 they expelled the Moors, in violation of their royal word pledged in the capitulations of Granada, they excepted those residing in Aragon, where Moorish agrarian manpower was indispensable for the farming of the noblemen's latifundia. On Isabella's accession and wilful defamation of her brother Henry IV and her niece Doña Juana, to shield her usurpation, see O. Ferrara, *Un pleito sucesorio. Enrique IV, Isabel de Castilla y la Beltraneja*, Madrid, 1945.

tions the legend of the magician Virgil whom — according to medieval legend — the Emperor's daughter had publicly humiliated. Her interlocutor remarks: "What you say is true, but that was not through justice," and Celestina, playing on the dual meaning of the word "justice" (namely 'judicial power' in general, and 'civil judicial power' in particular), replies: "Quiet, fool. You know little about the church's ways, and how much better it is to be punished by the hand of justice than *otherwise*." As a converted Jew, whose family had been persecuted by the Inquisition, and as a jurist, Bachelor Rojas well knew how much heavier was the hand of the so-called Holy Office than that of ordinary civil justice.

After reviewing the intellectual, religious, and political conflicts of England in Shakespeare's time, the English critic Theodore Spenser observes: "Nothing could have been more propitious for the writing of great tragic drama. In the periods when great tragedy has been written, two things seem to have been necessary: first, a conventional pattern of belief and behavior, and second, an acute consciousness of how that conventional pattern can be violated."[12] These conditions are fulfilled to the ultimate degree for the young convert Fernando de Rojas, and the Prologue which he added to the definitive edition of his work in 1502 leaves no doubt as to the world view underlying the *Tragicomedy*. It is a strange prologue; to tell us that the reaction to his work has been varied, Rojas spends three quarters of the space paraphrasing Petrarch's reflections on an aphorism by Heraclitus: in nature, he says, each thing fights the rest, and all are against us; as for man, his whole life is a senseless war against other men and against himself. Reading only the Prologue one may deem such an introduction inopportune and out of all proportion; reading the whole work, one notices its deep harmony with the *Tragicomedy*, and one understands Rojas' urgent desire to express it.[13] From the anguished vantage-point of a man in conflict with the tradition of his elders, which he has been forced to renounce, and with an imposed tradition,

[11] Only the humble convert Antón de Montoro, a poet called not without reason Spain's fifteenth-century Heine, informs Queen Isabella, bitterly laughing at himself, of the unceasing sacrifice that daily life was for the "new Christian" — a sacrifice brutally rejected by most "old Christians"; see *Cancionero*, edited by E. Cotarelo y Mori, Madrid, 1900, No. XXXVI, pp. 99-100.

[12] *Shakespeare and the Nature of Man*, New York, 1942, p. 50.

[13] This was perceived by the author of *An Interlude of Calisto and Melebea* (printed by John Rastell in London, ca. 1525), a play which opens with Melebea's speech summarizing the thoughts in Rojas' Prologue, and applying them to the characters; see reprint of the *Interlude* in H. Warner Allen's edition of James Mabbe's *The Spanish Bawd*, p. 267.

into which he finds no easy access, the convert Rojas observes society, sarcastically underlining its contradictions, its prejudices and its conventions. Rojas, the jurist, describes how characteristic it is of a good attorney to win the confidence of his client by using feigned arguments and much pacing back and forth before the judge (III, 132); the go-between Celestina, longing for the good old days, recalls how, as she entered the church, she was paid reverence by "clergymen of all ranks from bishops to sextons" (IX, 47). Another character scandalized throws in: "Surely not all of them!" and the old woman elaborates: "No, my son, and God forbid that I should say such a thing. For there were many pious old men with whom I had little success, and who even couldn't stand the sight of me, but I believe that it was out of sheer envy of those who spoke to me." In this society in which life, respectability and material possessions depended upon the observance of the State religion, no conventional or paradoxical ingredient of it escaped the critical eye of the convert. Rojas incarnated in the young nobleman Calisto the courtier's religiousness, which delighted in the erotic use of devout terminology. Melibea's devotion is more intimate and austere, but it stops her neither from deceiving her parents, nor from yielding to her love and, finally, committing suicide.[14] No more positive is the devotion of her father, Pleberio, for whom the world is a cruel chaos without a providential plan, or hope of immortality. Impeccably orthodox is the religiousness of the go-between Celestina and her girls, the only characters who think hopefully about their place in Paradise, and yet their piety falls short of keeping them from their no less sincere cultivation of witchcraft, and from their infamous traffic.

Equally typical of the critical detachment of the convert Rojas is his reaction to the concept of honor, the key to Castilian society, and from medieval times on, understood as a social rather than a moral sanction. In the *Tragicomedy*, the nobleman Calisto recalls his honor when he ponders over his conduct during the moment of repentance following the first satisfaction of his love; once this moment is past, he frees himself of his obligation to honor with a lack of concern that must have shocked readers of his time. Melibea does think sadly of her honor only to sacrifice it to her love. Her father, unlike the hard and revengeful father of the Golden Age *comedia*, after hearing her

---

[14] The *Interlude* affords an illuminating contrast: its author, intent on his moral message, causes Melebea to cut short her love affair thanks to her habit of daily prayer and work — an alteration which doubtless satisfied his didactic purpose, though at the cost of wrecking the drama.

confession, utters no word of reproach: he is too deeply immersed in his personal sorrow to care about the sanction of society. The noblemen, then, put passion before honor, but paradoxically, their servants remind them of their duty. It is, for instance, Melibea's humble maid who, on seeing her distraught by Calisto's death, forces her to regain her composure saying (XIX, 201): "Have the strength to bear the sorrow, as you had the daring to take the pleasure." And it is Celestina, even the go-between Celestina, who is most consciously proud of her professional honor for which she risks her life. As if the irony were not clear enough, the 1502 edition lets the braggart Centurio also flaunt his professional honor and pretend that he is ready to uphold at his sword's point the honor of the woman who keeps him, thus turning into mockery the very concept of honor.

With this desolate vision Rojas built his drama, a drama lacking heroes or villains, a struggle of equally destructive egoisms: the egoistic love of two enamored nobles, the egoistic avarice of a handful of servants, the egoistic rancor of a couple of prostitutes. Nothing is taken for granted, neither social nor literary convention. Rojas rejects lucky coincidence, the helpful stock-in-trade of the playwright ancient and modern. One happening leads to another in rigorous causal concatenation, although with unpredictable effects, and its total design shows the play of an irony which cruelly foils human intentions. The absence of stock situations is matched by an absence of stock characters, and Rojas audaciously sets his individual creatures against their corresponding archetypes. The young nobleman, all passion, is morbidly selfish and, at times, slightly ridiculous; the young girl in love who vindicates her passion with voluntary death, lies from her first to her last action; the servants, unlike the sagacious slaves of the Roman comedy and the servants of the Modern Age comedy, mere tools of their masters, live here a full and independent life; some are foolish, others discreet, some faithful, others treacherous, some dissolute, others austere. In short, Rojas has mustered the unprecedented courage to pay as much attention to each of them as to their masters, and, as if this in itself were not incredibly revolutionary, in the 1502 edition Rojas tangles the passions of the servants with the destiny of the masters, and has the noble Calisto die through the vengeance schemed by his servants' paramours, who are envious of Melibea. It is as if we were to say: Romeo dies at the hands of Samson and Gregory, or Macbeth at the hands of his Porter. Understandably, neither Lope de Vega, nor Shakespeare, nor Racine conceived such interplay between social levels; to do so was only in the power of a convert who, feeling himself at the fringe or even outside of society, refused to recognize the logic of its castes and could thus afford to give equal artistic dignity to noblemen and commoners.

Free from conventions, Rojas, naturally enough, showed himself attached to the fundamental realism of Castilian literature, that is, the evocation of the particular and concrete, which is consummated for the first time in the *Tragicomedy,* in the creation of a whole string of individual characters and in the representation of space and time with a margin of freedom unknown even to the Spanish and English theaters of the modern age. But the cultural norm of the period imposed the imitation of Latin and Italian motifs on every literary work worthy of respect. In deference to this norm, Rojas' characters, like Shakespeare's, are in general more eloquent and erudite than the relatively inarticulate and semiliterate characters of our own theater; but very often erudition and eloquence are placed too at the service of the drama, to outline a character or accentuate a situation. Calisto's love, passionate and cerebral at the same time, is much more literary than Melibea's; Celestina is not sparing in ministering precepts to the others that she is incapable of following herself. Melibea's parents, full of wise saws, decide to marry her off without revealing their intentions to her, lest they scandalize her virginal innocence: the senile wisdom of their maxims ironically emphasizes the blindness of their situation. Rojas has read Boccaccio's *Fiammetta* but, renouncing literary convention, he shifts the introspection, the passivity, the sentimentality of the Italian heroine, to Calisto rather than to Melibea, who in contrast with him appears active and determined.

The *Book of Good Love,* like so many medieval poems, draws a rhetorical portrait of the beloved woman: blond hair, wide forehead, clear eyes, etc. In Act I, the unknown author presents Calisto going over the details of this picture of his beloved, to the great boredom of the servant, who has no choice but to listen to him. Such ironic treatment was not enough for Rojas, and for this reason he contrasted the lover's enraptured description with the caricature of the same Melibea drawn by the loose women who envy her (IX, 32 ff.). The caricature derives from the book in which a moralist of the preceding generation, Alfonso Martínez de Toledo, Archpriest of Talavera, had satirically outlined various types of women: the avaricious, the inconstant, the disobedient, the envious; but in the *Tragicomedy* there are no abstract types; the malicious portrait in question arises dramatically, as the personal expression of the courtesans' resentment. The abundant lyrical production of the late fifteenth century also enters into the drama not as a conventional adornment, but dramatically, in order to delineate the characters as individuals and as members of society. Calisto recites polished verses of courtly poetry, or composes them; his servant sings some lines from a ballad, a literary form which the sophisticated persons of the time disdained; Melibea intones pastoral songs, in which merge echoes of Virgil's *Eclogues* with folk songs which are very much alive even today.

In the Spain that we associate with the turn of the sixteenth century, the sinister Spain of Torquemada, Bachelor Fernando de Rojas, who *was* under suspicion, could not take for granted the order of the world and of man and all the related conventions, as they had been taken for granted by Juan Ruiz, Archpriest of Hita, around the middle of the fourteenth century, a poet sure of the personal protection of the Virgin and closely attached to his ecclesiastical hierarchy. In the hands of the convert Rojas, the Latin comedy *Pamphilus,* good-humoredly re-worked by Juan Ruiz, was transformed into a tragedy — almost the only one creditable to Spanish literature, since tragedy was hardly possible, given the rigid thinking of the Golden Age. Instead of leading to the trite wedding of the young lovers, the work ends with the lament of Melibea's father, who feels impotent before the utter disorder of the world and the cruelty of love, without resignation and without consolation in the lonesomeness of his old age. Except for a few external facts, we know nothing about Fernando de Rojas, the principal author of *The Celestina,* but we do know this fact of primary importance which concerns the biography of his mind: at the most critical juncture of the history of Spanish Jews, Rojas the individual was crushed under a mortal anguish, an anguish which Rojas the artist sublimated in the creation of his *Tragicomedy of Calisto and Melibea.*

CHAPTER TWO

The *Book of Good Love:* Content, Genre, Purpose

The great Spanish poems of the twelfth and thirteenth centuries, though vigorously original, have their counterparts in other European literatures: the Spanish *Lay of the Cid* is comparable, for example, to the *Song of Roland,* the Spanish *Book of Alexander* to the German epics about the same hero. But the *Book of Good Love* has no pendant in any other literature of Western Europe. This fact has in no small way detracted from its appreciation, because the concepts put to use by literary criticism have been fashioned by analyzing the standard European production and, consequently, are quite unsuitable for apprehending what is atypical of it.

Now, aside from a Prologue in prose, added in the 1343 version, the elements of the *Book of Good Love* include: (a) a novel in autobiographical form, repeatedly interrupted, which serves as a frame-story for (b) a series of tales and fables; (c) a large number of didactic disquisitions on civil and canonic law (stanzas 221 ff., 1131 ff.), on points of literature and music (Prologue, stanzas 15, 65 ff., 1228, 1634 ff.), on love and morals, moral teachings being scattered throughout the entire work. Additional elements are (d) a free version of *Pamphilus* (a twelfth century Latin comedy); (e) an allegorical story of the battle between Sir Carnal and Lady Lent, and the triumph of Sir Love; (f) a miscellany of lyrical poems: the devotional ones being almost all songs to the Virgin; the worldly ones comprise a mocking song and four burlesque pastourelles (all of them lyrical variations on themes previously expressed in narrative verse), and songs for blind men and mendicant students.

Of all these elements, the most important from the structural viewpoint is the autobiographical novel, which narrates thirteen amorous adventures, curiously similar; the locale is in nine cases the town and in four the *sierras.* In the town, the poet proffers verses and gifts through his messengers to various loves, among them a baker woman, a pious widow, a nun, a Moorish girl; all his efforts are of no avail.

18

In the *sierras,* four enterprising mountain lasses try to make love to him: twice the poet manages to dodge them, twice he falls prey to the shrews; the result is always the same — a defeat exposing him to ridicule. Obviously, this is not a closed novel, with an exposition, a climax, and a conclusion, moving around a central action or a psychological trajectory of a character, as the modern novels of Balzac, Dickens, or Tolstoy. If it invites comparison with something, it is with the Spanish novel of the Golden Age — a century in which Juan Ruiz was totally unknown — the picaresque novel and *Don Quixote,* whose protagonists give unity to a succession of parallel adventures in which they always end up in an unenviable position.

What is the significance of this autobiographical frame-story? For the naïve reader it is an authentic record historically true. In addition to the scribe of the latest manuscript, various Spanish critics of our time maintain that much of what the *Book of Good Love* narrates in the first person actually happened to the man Juan Ruiz, since he recounts it "with a realistic criterion." The truth is that with that same "realistic criterion" the poet reports his colloquies with Sir Love, with Lady Venus, and with Sir Carnal; moreover, the "biography" thus inferred from the poem turns out to be a fabric of unedifying adventures having among themselves a similarity quite remote from the variety of life, and finally, in two key passages, on commenting upon the longest episode, and on concluding the *Book,* the poet addresses his public and solemnly avers (909ab and 1634bc):

> And realize full well I spin my tale of Lady Sloe
> To teach a moral, not because it happened to me so . . .

> this my poem has been writ
> To check the wrongs and injuries which persons ill commit.[1]

The individual, Juan Ruiz, figures frequently in the poem, but this autobiography is no narration of his personal history. Autobiography, written directly, in the first person, was very rare in Western Europe, both in Antiquity and in the Middle Ages.[2] In the vernacular litera-

---

[1] Kane's translation, slightly modified in stanza 1634b. "Lady Sloe" [*doña Endrina*].

[2] A few examples could be culled from Hellenistic and Roman literature, such as Petronius', Apuleius', and Lucian's autobiographical fiction (see G. Misch, *A History of Autobiography in Antiquity,* transl. by E. W. Dickes, Cambridge, Mass., 1951, which however focuses more on autobiographical content than on autobiography as a literary genre), but it may be safely assumed that Juan Ruiz had no inkling of such authors. He shows no knowledge even of Saint Augustine's *Confessions* and Boethius' *Consolation of Philosophy,* two autobiographical works then widely read. Two considerations alert us to the medieval aloofness from autobiography: (1) when Cassiodorus

tures it remained unknown, I think, until the thirteenth century, when Ulrich von Lichtenstein wrote his *Frauendienst,* followed by Dante's *Vita Nuova,* so that the fictitious use of the autobiographical form was not natural as it would have been after the Renaissance, and above all, after the Romantic movement. Moreover, the *Frauendienst* and the *Vita Nuova* unfold a chain of dissimilar events and dynamically outline the character of the respective protagonist; Dante, above all, whatever the relationship between truth and fantasy may be, not only builds his book around his love for Beatrice, but also around the irreversible growth of his own character. His reactions on the last page cannot be confused with those of the first, very much in contrast to what happens in the *Book of Good Love* — and even in *Don Quixote:* Juan Ruiz, like Cervantes, absent-mindedly quotes as already written an episode which has not yet appeared, for the simple reason that the episodes are essentially repeated actions implying no psychological development nor causal relationship in time.[3]

Within the Christian environment of mid-fourteenth-century Spain, the autobiography of the *Book of Good Love* is entirely unique. For this reason, in 1894 the Arabist Francisco Fernández y González identified the poem, in terms of literary genre, with the Semitic *maqāmāt.* This genre was created in the tenth century by al-Hamadhani (an Arabic author, born in Persia, the same man who created the song for blind men, cultivated by Juan Ruiz), and perfected in the

(ca. 490-583) had Josephus' works translated into Latin, he omitted the historian's *Life,* one of the all too rare autobiographies transmitted from Antiquity, as if this writing made no sense to him; (2) when Guibert de Nogent (1053-1124) composed *De vita sua,* he adopted a style far less elaborate than his own style used in his historical works and, after Book I, abandoned the autobiographical narrative, except for a few passages, and objectively narrated the events in Nogent and in Laon. While his religious and historical treatises have come down in numerous MSS, *De vita sua* has been preserved in a single modern copy because, as its editor remarks "l'œuvre de Guibert ne rentrait pas dans les genres littéraires admis du moyen-âge" (Guibert de Nogent, *Histoire de sa vie;* ed. G. Bourgin, Paris, 1907, p. xxxv). P. Lehmann, "Autobiographies of the Middle Ages," *Transactions of the Royal Historical Society,* Fifth Series, III (1953), 41-52, points out that Saint Augustine's *Confessions and Retractations* "were widely copied, read and used in the Middle Ages, but were neither of them ever effectively imitated" (p. 42; cf. p. 46), and that even in confessions written in the ecclesiastical sense, "the individual autobiographical touch is normally avoided" (p. 43).

[3] In the *Book of Good Love,* 1323c, Dame Convent-trotter, the procuress, alludes to her fruitless conversation with the Moorish girl, a passage which in all extant MSS, occurs only in stanzas 1508-12. Compare the report on the three lawsuits judged by Sancho in *Don Quixote,* Part II, Ch. xlv: to praise Sancho's verdict in the first (the case of the five caps), Cervantes asserts that it was more admired than the sentence he had pronounced in the case of the drover's purse — which, in fact, is the third lawsuit.

eleventh by al-Hariri, likewise a Persian Arab. In the *maqāmāt* a rogue preaches a virtue and piety which he is far from practicing. A master of grammar, rhetoric, poetry and schemes for thriving at the cost of his neighbor, he declaims in sessions (i.e., *maqāmāt*) where the narrator repeatedly confronts the rogue and reports in the first person the latter's deviltry (of which he, the narrator, is at times the victim), and transmits as well the rogue's declamations. These two persons give unity to the different adventures, set in bourgeois surroundings and expressed in rhymed prose with the interpolation of lyric poems, of debates and disquisitions on moral and erudite themes, in a style which is a display of verbal pyrotechnics. All this agrees remarkably with the *Book of Good Love,* but these Arabic *maqāmāt* differ in that their poems are not variations on earlier narratives, they contain no tales or fables, and hardly touch the love theme. Also their two characters are as far removed from the single "I," which links the *Book of Good Love,* as al-Hamadhani and al-Hariri, Arabs from Persia, are removed from Juan Ruiz's Spain.

From the twelfth to the fourteenth centuries, the Jews of Catalonia, Languedoc, and Provence, informed by a non-traditional and lay orientation and, consequently, sympathetic with the Arabic art and science, assiduously cultivated the *maqāmāt,* reworking them with great originality. If we compare the masterpiece of the Hispano-Hebraic *maqāmāt,* the *Tahkemoni* by Yehuda ben Selomo al-Harisi (between the twelfth and thirteenth centuries) with Arabic *maqāmāt,* we realize that the Jew coincides with Juan Ruiz in profusely commenting on the origin of his book, on its literary and moral intention, contents and merits, amid alternate professions of mastery and modesty. He further coincides with Juan Ruiz in that his hero is not a rogue, and that the inserted poems are lyrical variations on the subject-matter previously dealt with in a narrative form. A second example of the Hispano-Hebraic *maqāmāt* shows radical departures from the Arabic model, which are so many steps in the direction of the *Book of Good Love:* I refer to the *Book of Delights*[4] by the physician from Barcelona, Yosef ben Meir ibn Zabarra (second half of the twelfth century), a work in which the protagonist and narrator appear fused into one character, identified with the author. He, exactly as Juan Ruiz, is the protagonist of a single, rather loose narration, functioning as a frame-story for debates, dissertations, aphorisms, proverbs, por-

[4] English translation by Moses Hadas, New York, 1932. I. González-Llubera's Catalan translation (Barcelona, 1931), with excellent Introduction and notes, also deserves consultation.

traits, parodies, tales and fables which, in turn, may introduce other tales and fables. The *Book of Delights* begins and ends with explanatory pieces and dedications in lyric verse at the beginning and in rhymed prose at the end, characteristics which recall the 1330 version of the *Book of Good Love,* with its initial lyrics to the Virgin and its epilogue in narrative verse. The narrator-protagonist reports that there appeared to him, a giant, his future interlocutor throughout the rest of the work, a situation which recalls the appearance of Sir Love as "a tall man" (181c), who is Juan Ruiz's interlocutor in the most important debate in his poem. The giant, with all kinds of promises, offers to conduct Yosef to his city. After a long deliberation for and against trips, comparable to Juan Ruiz's deliberation for and against love, Yosef accepts, just as after the debate with Sir Love, the Archpriest starts his longest episode. The wanderings of the two travelers bring to mind Juan Ruiz's journeys through the cities and across mountains. Finally, Yosef's displeasure with the unfamiliar city and nostalgia for his native land recall the line in which the lonely Juan Ruiz, passing through the city of Segovia, expresses the nostalgia for his home — that exquisite line which stirred Azorín's imagination (973b):[5]

> Neither well of waters fresh, nor eternal source I found.

Such is the skeleton of the autobiographical narrative in the *Book of Delights;* to the similarities already indicated, we should add an equal taste for reminiscences of the Scriptures, a tract on physiognomy, the caricature of an ugly woman, a humoristic portrait based on antithesis and verbal paradox, an invective against wine, a series of vilifications of the interlocutor, strung not at his first appearance, but much later in a quarrel ending in a reconciliation — all of which have their exact counterparts in the *Book of Good Love.* There are also various jokes common to both works; let me mention only one. Yosef reports that Socrates, married to a petite woman, apologized: "I have chosen the least of evil." On finishing the droll sermon "Concerning the qualities which little women have" Juan Ruiz counsels his audience (1617cd):

> Now of two evils choose the less, — said a wise man of the East,
> By consequence, of woman-kind be sure to choose the least.[6]

Into this fictitious autobiography — and the long intervention of a supernatural interlocutor, the giant or Sir Love, underlines its ficti-

---

[5] Azorín [José Martínez Ruiz], *Al margen de los clásicos* [Marginalia on the Classics], Madrid, 1915, "Juan Ruiz," pp. 20 ff.

[6] Longfellow's translation, published in "Spanish Language and Literature" in *The North American Review,* April, 1833, and later included in *The Poets and Poetry of Europe.*

tious quality — the two authors introduce their personal learning, a pattern which explains why the dissertations are medical in the *Book of Delights* and ecclesiastic in the *Book of Good Love.* The obvious difference, in regard to the content, consists in that, although Yosef now and then treats of women, he refrains from narrating amorous episodes; but other Hispano-Hebraic *maqāmāt,* especially those of Selomo ibn Siqbal of Cordova, offer them, in the guise of repeated disappointments of the protagonist. It would be ill-advised to posit for Juan Ruiz the bookish imitation of the Hebrew *maqāmāt,* but the priceless confession: "Next after that I wrote the words to many a dancing song/For Jewesses," and his familiarity with the Ghetto, prove that specific knowledge of such works may well have reached him.

What remains to be asked is why Juan Ruiz chose this autobiographical structure and not the frame-story in the form of a tale including a cluster of other tales—as in the *Thousand and One Nights*— a form no doubt familiar to him from several Arabic collections translated into Castilian in the thirteenth and widely imitated in the fourteenth century. The truth is that if anything stands out in the *Book of Good Love* it is an exuberant, irrepressible personality, which refused to be satisfied with a frame-story barring the author from a personal appearance. Therefore, Juan Ruiz preferred the fictitious autobiography of the Hispano-Hebraic *maqāmāt,* which permitted him to step into the foreground of the narrative in order to proclaim his instructive experience, be it true or imaginary. For a proven way, apparently spontaneous, to enhance the pedagogical efficacy of any teaching, consists in presenting it as the teacher's personal experience. The Psalmist, objectively asserting that the good man suffers no poverty, affirms (XXXVII, 25): "*I* have been young, and now am old, yet have *I* not seen the righteous forsaken, nor his seed begging bread." Ovid — if you will excuse the medieval juxtaposition of the Scriptures and the *Art of Love* — teaches that the penniless lover cannot afford the luxury of indulging in bad temper, and he brings home the point with a personal anecdote (II, 169 ff.):

> Once in a rage her hair I towsed about.
> How many days that tantrum cut me out!
> I never felt . . . don't think . . . but she declared . . .
> I tore a frock; my purse the loss repaired.
> You, if you're shrewd, your *master's* errors flee:
> Shy from the damage my guilt brought to *me.*[7]

Summing up: the books that medieval learned men held dearest authorized the spontaneous habit of instructing in the first person,

[7] Translation by E. Phillips Barker, *The Lover's Manual,* Oxford, 1931.

a habit which no doubt confirmed Juan Ruiz in choosing the auto-biographical structure of the Hispano-Hebraic *maqāmāt* as a frame-story for his poem.

Concerning the didactic purpose that guided Juan Ruiz's pen, a heated controversy has been raging since the poem was first redis-covered. The reader of our days — I refer especially to the Hispanic reader — tolerates symbolic, indirect didacticism in the novel and in the theater: in poetry he categorically rejects it. Neither does he admit compromises and jests in moral and religious instruction, and condemns as antipedagogical any teaching through negative examples. For these reasons, many readers of the *Book of Good Love* challenge its didactic intention. Now, such reasons are ways or styles of our times: the resistance of those readers stems only from the fact that Juan Ruiz conducted himself as a fourteenth- and not as a twentieth-century man.

1. First of all, the didactic intent is not a conjecture; it follows from the poet's express and insistent declarations. Of course, every master-piece, once achieved, transcends the specific intent with which the author started: the *Aeneid* is much more than the glorification of Emperor Augustus, just as *Don Quixote* has outgrown the mere attack on the romances of chivalry. But an author's avowed point of de-parture is an invaluable datum, which one ought not to cast aside simply because it is not in harmony with present-day thinking. Juan Ruiz's declarations agree with many traits of his text; those critics, unwilling to take at their face value the author's declarations, must venture for these traits explanations extremely hazardous. True, an author may, more or less sincerely, attribute to his work, once it has been written, an intent which did not guide him while he was at work on it.[8] As for the Archpriest, he has stated his didactic aim in

[8] This, I believe, is the case of *The Celestina,* whose avowed didactic pur-pose ("in reprehension of foolish lovers . . . and advising against the deceits of go-betweens and of wicked and wheedling servants," I, p. 27) is far nar-rower and triter than the bitter message that flows from the work as a whole. In the Prologue to his *Exemplary Novels,* Cervantes announces: "I have called them *exemplary,* because, if you rightly consider them, there is not one of them from which you may not draw some useful example" (translation by Walter K. Kelly, London, 1855, p. x). There is no ground for disputing Cervantes' sincerity in the Prologue; yet, we may not unreasonably doubt that the reader's edification was foremost in his mind when he was describing with such gusto the doings of two lads who, instead of joining the university chosen by their fathers, embraced a rogue's life (*The Illustrious Scullery Maid*), the pleasant freedom of gypsies (*The Gypsy Girl*), and Seville's bizarrely organ-ized underworld (*Rinconete and Cortadillo*). For a full discussion of Juan Ruiz's didacticism, see "Nuevas notas para la interpretación del *Libro de buen amor,*" pp. 28-60.

his Prologue in prose, in the first 71 quatrains by way of introduction, at the beginning and the conclusion of many episodes (76, 105 ff., 161 ff., 892 ff., 944d, 950, 951d, 1319c, 1503 ff., 1508d), at random junctures (for example, 986cd, 1390cd), and in the final peroration. Obviously, his didactic purpose, far from being an afterthought, permeates the entire poem.

2. The *Book of Good Love* belongs to the literary genre of the Semitic *maqāmāt,* an essentially didactic genre. The teaching of the *maqāmāt* is, above all, moralizing; they also display the author's literary virtuosity and diversified knowledge, that is to say, those very same categories of teaching which the *Book of Good Love* offers. Experts in the history of Spanish law, music and poetry do, of course, draw on Juan Ruiz's declarations though, paradoxically, they are wont to reject the moral declarations which the poet points out as his most important didactic purpose. Moreover, and again following the model of the *maqāmāt,* the didacticism of the *Book of Good Love* expresses itself not only in the autobiographical novel serving as a framework, but also in the tales, fables and satires enclosed in this framework, all of which would be jarring appendages if they were divorced from the general didactic intent of the work.

3. The title of the poem, *Book of Good Love,*[9] corroborates the intention here assumed. Juan Ruiz formulates the title three times in the body of the work (13cd, 933ab, 1630ab), and the first time he indicates, leaving not a shadow of a doubt, that he aspires to the ideal of a didactic and, at the same time, aesthetically satisfying literature, for he asks God's aid

> That with Thy help my *Book of Good Love* may I write,
> A book to improve the soul and the body to delight.

At the second mention, the poet reports that to placate the old go-between with whom he has quarrelled, he calls her "Good Love"; and for the sake of his attachment to her he has given this title to the *Book,* although at the same time he adds (933a):

> and because it seemed right.

Does this joke prove that Juan Ruiz is not in earnest about the title and subject of his poem? Certainly not. Calling the agent of foolish love "Good Love" is a travesty no less obvious than imagining that the

---

[9] Ramón Menéndez Pidal, "Título que el Arcipreste de Hita dio al libro de sus poesías," *Revista de Archivos, Bibliotecas y Museos,* Serie III, II (1898), 106-109, has definitely shown that *Book of Good Love* [Libro de buen amor] is the authentic title. None is preserved at the beginning of the MSS, and in the fifteenth century the poem was quoted as "The Archpriest's Book" — a tribute to Juan Ruiz's striking personality.

sinful go-between dwells in Paradise among the martyrs (1570ab). But just as it would be unwarranted to infer from this last joke that Juan Ruiz failed to believe in Paradise or in the martyrs, so one must not infer from the first joke that he lacked any belief in the superior hierarchy of Good Love and in the purpose of his *Book* as a guide to it.

4. Various traits of structure, the presentation of characters, the style and meter are inherent in the didactic purpose. The most salient structural characteristic is the repetition of parallel episodes. The thirteen amorous adventures of the autobiographical novel, very similar to one another in their details and identical in their outcome, each frustrating the poet's desire, illustrate through their repeated failure the didactic thesis which Juan Ruiz explicitly sets forth when he muses on his first defeat (105):

> As King Solomon has said (and indeed he preaches true)
> All wordly things are vanity, all pass like morning dew,
> All things vanish through age, the ancient and the new,
> All things, save to love God, are frivolous to do.[10]

Moreover, there are various didactic passages which Juan Ruiz displays twice, very deliberately, since the later passages refer back to the earlier ones (608 ff. to 423 ff., 937 ff. to 699 ff., 1583 to 217 ff.), clear evidence that he feels so intensely the urge to impart his doctrine that he joyfully welcomes any opportunity to revert to it.

The presentation of the characters offers what at first sight seems a singular paradox: the more important the person, the less individualized he or she is. Not only do the personifications and mythological figures show this unusual trait, but the protagonist too. Though introducing himself by his name and profession, the protagonist affirms solemnly his universal nature when starting his autobiography, and repeats it with variations on beginning his sundry adventures (76a):

> So I, because I am a man, the same as any sinner.[11]

That is to say: I, Juan Ruiz, Archpriest of Hita, will tell of my love adventures not in the name of the individual man Juan Ruiz, not as personal and romantic confidences in the manner of Rousseau or of Goethe, but as a universal human confession: I will speak as the sinner that every man is, like the pilgrim Gonzalo de Berceo in the *Miracles of Our Lady* or *Everyman* in the morality-play of that title. To such a degree is this true that, when one of the ladies asks for the Archpriest's portrait, the description which follows is not individualized; rather it combines the generic marks which medieval

[10] The second hemistich of the last line is borrowed from Kane.
[11] Kane's translation.

doctors attributed to a sanguine temperament, that is, to a buoyant and sensual type of man. Neither is the picture of the go-between individualized; Sir Love describes what "these convent-trotters" are like in general (441d); then the protagonist evokes the particular Dame Convent-trotter who will figure in the *Book,* still subsuming her under the general type (699 ff.):

> A hawker was she, one of those who sell and peddle gauds,
> Those who lure girls to their traps, those who bait them
>   with frauds . . .[12]

The same thing happens to the women loved by the protagonist: the poet praises their beauty or their nobility in the most general terms; even when describing at some length Lady Sloe and Lady Garoza (653, 1499bc and 1502a), the descriptions share some common traits, and suspiciously coincide with the archetype of loveliness sketched earlier by Sir Love (432 ff.). The detailed portrait of one of the mountain lasses is not individual either: it is a caricature which fuses all the conceivable features of feminine ugliness, a rhetorical exercise which was not infrequent in the Middle Ages: witness the parallel mentioned in the *Book of Delights,* and others, for instance in the French prose *Perceval,* in *Sir Gawain and the Green Knight,* in Skelton's "The Tunning of Elinour Rumming." On the other hand, Juan Ruiz individualizes with conspicuous vigor the quite secondary figures introduced in comparisons and descriptions: the dancing girl and the weaver, who cannot keep their feet still, the one while operating the loom, the other at the sound of the tambourine (470 ff.); or the month of June, personified as a peasant who "had eaten unripe grapes, and now his voice was hoarse," while "his hands were stained full red, as there was such plenty of cherries" (1290 f.).

Now, this discrepancy is inherent in the didactic literature of all times. The fable, or the theater of types, do not individualize the fox, the wolf, the miser, the hypocrite, precisely because they aim to present them as conventional typifications of human conduct, but authors who are great artists — fabulists like Juan Ruiz, Don Juan Manuel, Lope de Vega, La Fontaine; dramatists like Alarcón, Ben Jonson, Molière — enrich their didactic works with the concreteness they have freely observed outside the conventional typification of the genre.[13]

---

[12] Kane's translation slightly modified. This and other didactic features have been pointed out by the late L. Spitzer, "Zur Auffassung der Kunst des Arcipreste de Hita," *Zeitschrift für romanische Philologie,* LIV (1934), 237-270, though not in connection with the *maqāmāt.*

[13] Note that even though Juan Ruiz's descriptions of his animal protagonists vastly surpass those by most fabulists (witness the portrayal of the over-

Since the didactic purpose is the kernel of the *Book of Good Love* and is not an appendage to it, it also appears in its style. Thus, each concrete episode has a general range of application (76, 260, 592), each character is ascribed to a category (433cd, 699a); each thought is referred to a learned text which lends it authority (44a, 446c); the numerous sayings and proverbs add weight to the end of the stanza; above all, we notice the typical procedure of the educator and of the preacher: the variation on a given theme which, as a matter of fact, is the essential technique of the poem. Finally, it should be remembered that the metric form prevailing in the *Book of Good Love* is the "fourfold way" [*quaderna vía*], a monorhyme quatrain with lines oscillating between fourteen and sixteen syllables. It had been introduced into Spain in the preceding century by ecclesiastic poets who, for the enlightenment of the lay public, composed in the vernacular those narratives which the clerics had all along been reading in Latin. That is, it had been introduced by a poetic school of markedly didactic aims.

5. The most extensive episode in the *Book of Good Love* is a brilliant paraphrase of the twelfth-century Latin comedy, *Pamphilus;* very significant is the fact that Juan Ruiz injected his didactic preoccupation into this foreign material. (a) As the comedy was the story of a seduction which ended in marriage, Juan Ruiz has added on his own a long moralization, the longest in the poem, evidently as a foil to the happy ending. (b) Compared with the Old Woman in *Pamphilus,* Dame Convent-trotter is a much livelier figure. Even so, Juan Ruiz — hemmed in by the typification inherent in didactic literature — limits himself to developing a single aspect of her character: the mastery of the arts leading to foolish love, the only aspect he intends to censure severely. On the other hand, Fernando de Rojas shapes his Celestina as a multi-faceted personage because, having shed didactic typification, he aims to present an integral human creature. Or, to put it differently: Celestina is a character in a drama; Dame Convent-trotter is a character in a fable. (c) In the Latin original the protagonists bear classical names: Pamphilus, borrowed from the comedies of Terence; Galatea, from the *Eclogues* of Virgil. Juan Ruiz rejects the ornate ancient names, rich in esthetic and erudite connotations, and replaces them with morally significant Spanish names. He does so not in the abstract manner of Langland, Ben

worked horse, 242 f.), he is at his very best when sketching animals in comparisons or in brief, secondary evocations (cf. 563b: the peacock; 569c: the heron; 1092a: the old ox; 1219b: the greyhound; 1293cd: the gad-fly, etc.).

Jonson or Bunyan, but rather in a very personal manner, halfway between the metaphor and the proverb: Pamphilus becomes Sir Melon; Galatea, Lady Sloe. Sir Melon, because in popular parlance the melon symbolizes especially persons (or things) with whom success depends not on careful choice but on chance, a view underlying the saw: "In melons and marriages one depends on a chance hit."[14] Lady Sloe, because the sloe is the wild downy plum symbolic of the delicacy of feminine honor. A later poet embroiders: "A maid is like the sloe, which even if scarcely touched shows the fingers' mark."[15] The substitution for the lovely ancient names of these popular ones, at once jocose and moralizing, served the purpose of alerting the public from the start to the didactic significance of the characters.

6. Today's reader, unfamiliar with medieval mentality, finds it difficult to take seriously a moral teaching which, in order to preach divine love, assiduously inserts case-histories of worldly love. But this procedure was dogma for medieval pedagogy, relying upon Saint Paul's precept to the Thessalonians (I, 21), with which Juan Ruiz heads his autobiography (76cd) and the narrative of his adventures in the *sierras* (950a) :

> No harm is done to man by putting things to test,
> By knowing good and evil, choosing from all the best.[16]

The basis of teaching through fables is no different, since the predominant moral is the one which admonishes: "Do not act like the grasshopper," "Do not act like the crow." Nor is there any departure in the principle pervading the Spanish picaresque novel, the most

[14] "El melón y el casamiento ha de ser acertamiento."

[15] Luis Quiñones de Benavente, *Entremés de Pipote* (E. Cotarelo y Mori, *Colección de entremeses,* Madrid, 1911, I, 2, *Nueva Biblioteca de Autores Españoles,* XVIII, p. 715a, No. 301): "que también la doncella es como endrina, / que apenas la han tocado / cuando el dedo le dejan señalado."

[16] Many, of course, forgot the second half of the precept, as the lady in William Langland, *The Vision of Piers the Plowman,* Passus III, v. 334 ff. (done into modern English by W. W. Skeat, London, 1922): "Thou'rt like a lady that read once a lesson, 'Twas 'prove ye well all things,' and pleased was her heart, For the line was no longer, at the end of the leaf. Had she looked any longer or turned the leaf over, More words had she found there, that follow close after, 'Hold fast what is good.'" As far as I know, the first Spanish moralist to oppose the medieval teaching of wisdom by exhibiting folly was Fray Juan de Pineda, *Diálogos de la agricultura cristiana* [Dialogues on Christian Agriculture], Salamanca, 1589, I, xxii, 25. Apropos of the alleged moral purpose of *The Celestina,* Pineda argued that it was by far safer not to awaken the reader's sensuality, than to incite it by a too lively artistic presentation of vice.

typical of which (*Guzmán de Alfarache*) is subtitled *"The Watch-tower of Human Life,"* and, according to some laudatory verses,

> teaches
> By its opposite example
> How to lead a righteous life.

The same applies to Cervantes' *Exemplary Novels* and to their seventeenth-century imitations, to the comedy of types and to the thesis plays of more recent vintage, let us say Bertolt Brecht's dramas depicting life in Nazi Germany, or Arthur Miller's *The Crucible,* centering about the persecution of witches in Salem.

The habit of presenting moral and religious teachings in a facetious way goes against the grain of the modern reader, but the medieval authors who advocate and practice this device are too numerous to be cited.[17] Moreover, as the notion of what is facetious and decorous has notably changed through six centuries, it happens that at times episodes now classified as risqué could very well have been used without hypocrisy in order to impart edifying lessons. This habit, so shocking for us, disappeared — not in a day. Suffice it to recall that toward the middle of the sixteenth century, Marguerite de Valois, Queen of Navarre, a princess of unimpeachable conduct, pious, mystically inclined, and even very much concerned with the orthodox reform of Catholicism, wrote — not in her youth but in her last years — the *Heptaméron,* a collection of tales, lewd and scatological in the main, whose edifying message she relentlessly expounds.[18]

7. The habit of making an abstract lesson palpable by means of a jocular story received support also from the allegorical exegesis of the Scriptures, obligatory in the Middle Ages for Jews, Christians and Muslims alike. In accord with this precedent, any respected text could be allegorized, i.e., the medieval reader was bound to discover in it what he was striving to discover. Thus, Chrétien Legouais, John

---

[17] To the Arabic authors favoring the alternation of comic and serious matters, quoted by Castro, *La realidad histórica de España,* pp. 282 and 415, add the Christian counterparts identified by Otis H. Green, "On Juan Ruiz's Parody of the Canonical Hours," *Hispanic Review,* XXVI (1953), 13.

[18] See P. Jourda, *Marguerite d'Angoulême,* Paris, 1930, II, pp. 887, 911, and more especially E. V. Telle, *L'Œuvre de Marguerite d'Angoulême, Reine de Navarre, et la Querelle des Femmes,* Toulouse, 1937, pp. 94, 139-145, and L. Febvre, *Autour de l'Heptaméron; amour sacré, amour profane,* Paris, 1944, pp. 208-213. A case in point is the widespread medieval practice of enlivening sermons with stories and fables, a practice first prohibited by the Council of Bordeaux, 1624. The celebrated Bavarian preacher Abraham a Sancta Clara (1644-1709) still upheld religious teaching by means of scurrilous tales and parody: see T. G. von Karajan, *Abraham a Sancta Clara,* Vienna, 1867, pp. 234, 241 f., and G. Highet, *The Classical Tradition,* New York, 1949, pp. 308, 649.

of Garland and a host of other medieval worthies, read into Ovid's *Metamorphoses* all they knew about Biblical history and Christian morals. Conversely, the writer felt authorized to compose stories totally devoid of austerity, and to point out later that, aside from the literal, purely entertaining meaning, the reader could detect other more valuable meanings, in harmony with his moral and intellectual capacity. Such a concept of the book, and its various layers of meaning, dependent upon the merit of the reader, befits the medieval vision of the world. This philosophy regards all creation as valuable, but hierarchized with respect to the Creator, on a scale which goes from worldly pleasure to ascetic renunciation, from carnal lovemaking to divine love. Just as man chooses freely and responsibly, according to his degree of insight, the best or the worst possibility of all those which the world offers him, so the reader, equally responsible for his selection, is free to open a book at the profitable or at the frivolous page; he may content himself with the frivolous literal meaning or search for the profitable allegorical meaning. It would be an easy matter to illustrate these ideas with works as significant as the treatise *The Art of Courtly Love* by Andreas Capellanus, Boccaccio's *Decamerone* and Chaucer's *Canterbury Tales*. In his *maqāmāt* the Arab al-Hariri, addressing the unlettered and coarse-minded reader, insists upon the moral value of his work — which the discreet reader will understand and judge on a par with fables and apologues. In the Prologue to his *Tahkemoni,* the Spanish Jew Yehuda ben Selomo al-Harisi declares:

You may liken this book to a garden where all kinds of flowers are to be found. It offers to everyone that which he desires; grants to everyone that which he yearns for, according to his nature and learning, according to his capacity and aptitude. Whoever reveres the word of God, learns there to fear God. Whoever pays no attention to it, can apply himself to the earthly matters which it contains. From its vast scope the fool and the sage, the young and the old, may benefit, each in a different way.

Thus we understand how Juan Ruiz could write in all earnest that in the gay stories of his *Book* the reader "of sound judgement, eager to be saved, will choose and act accordingly," while the sinner will find instructions for sinning (Prologue, p. 6):

And thus this book of mine, for every man or woman, wise or unwise, whether he perceives the good and perceives the way to salvation and works through loving God well, or otherwise desires worldly love, in whatsoever direction he may go, each one may well say, "I shall give thee understanding."[19]

[19] Kane's translation, pp. 4 f. The quotation is taken from Psalm 31:8, verse 8 being the Biblical authority for the whole Prologue.

This attitude is to such an extent the key to the *Book of Good Love* that Juan Ruiz, not satisfied with expounding it in his Prologue and Epilogue and alluding to it in several passages, interpolates as a guide, before entering upon the autobiographical frame-story, a delightful apologue, the "Disputation between Greeks and Romans" (44 ff.). The Romans asked the Greeks for laws, the latter laid down as a preliminary condition a disputation, and by request of the Romans, who spoke no Greek, agreed to carry it on by signs. Lacking wise men, the aggrieved Romans took a knave:

> In a dress of finest cloth well and richly attired was he,
> As a teacher of Philosophy, with a doctoral degree.

When the moment arrived, the wisest among the doctors of Greece stood up and raised his index finger; the knave very fiercely showed his index, middle finger, and thumb; the Greek extended his palm; the Roman showed his fist. The Greek doctor, then, declared himself highly satisfied with the wisdom of the Romans since, he explained, when he raised one finger to indicate that God is one, the Roman raised three to indicate that He has three persons; when he extended his palm to show that the world is under His will, the Roman showed his fist, meaning that God has the world in His power. When the knave was questioned, he in turn explained: "The Greek told me that he would split my eye with one finger; I answered him that I would smash his teeth with one finger and that with the other two I would poke out his eyes; then he told me that he would box my ears; and I promised to give him such a blow that he would never be able to avenge it, and then he stopped threatening me." Indeed, the sign has many meanings. All its meanings are admissible, but not all are equally valuable; the vulgar meaning which the knave chooses in accordance with his knavery is inferior to the theological meaning which the doctor chooses in accordance with his wisdom and learning.

In short, the *Book of Good Love,* a work of *mudéjar* art, fits its Christian motifs into the structure of the Hispano-Hebraic *maqāmāt.* As a result, it is an artistic composition with a didactic purpose, which above all proposes to inculcate precepts of moral behavior, and to that end utilizes the autobiography of the author who acts as protagonist and teacher, repeatedly heaping ridicule on himself so as to warn the public against his own moral misconduct. In Juan Ruiz's century and in the following one, his doctrinal intention lost him no sympathizers. All the early quotations (down to 1450) correspond to didactic passages, while none of the various lacunae and omissions which mar the extant text has damaged those moral passages. Don Ramón Menéndez Pidal, the great master of Spanish philology, has discovered a curious manuscript containing some kind of outline or program for a minstrel recitation of about 1420. In that program, the minstrel

on feeling the interest of his audience wane, stirred it with magic words: "Now let us begin the *Book* of the Archpriest," certain that this simple announcement would make his listeners rejoice in advance, expecting a thousand fanciful stories of townspeople and mountain lasses, of scurrilous lampoons, skillful fables, inimitable imitations of Pamphilus and Ovid, and songs and ballads.[20]

The illustrious critic has omitted from this list every didactic element, doubtless because it happens to run contrary to present-day taste, but what the minstrel in fact recites after the magic words "Now let us begin the *Book* of the Archpriest" is a couple of moralizing passages upon the evils of excessive drinking and upon the power of money. After all, why should *we* impose our twentieth-century tastes and prejudices on a poet of the fourteenth century and his immediate audiences?

[20] Menéndez Pidal, *Poesía juglaresca y orígenes de las literaturas románicas,* Madrid, 1957, p. 209; cf. 234 ff.

CHAPTER THREE

"Now let us begin the Book
of the Archpriest"

So far we have spoken of the author and his environment, of the content, structure, and purpose of the *Book of Good Love*. Following in the footsteps of the fifteenth-century minstrel, I will continue with the "magic words": "Now let us begin the Book of the Archpriest." Let us then run through the poem in its definitive version, pausing only at a few passages, the most successful in the original and the least maimed in the translations.[1]

You recall that the *Book* — written by and large in the "fourfold way," that is, in monorhymed quatrains with lines oscillating between fourteen and sixteen syllables — begins with a prayer to God and to the Virgin. A Prologue in prose next points out the various levels of the book. There follows an invocation in verse, probably the Prologue of the first version, which applies to the poem the contrast, eminently

[1] Owing to its predominantly subjective, intuitive and popular character, Spanish literature does not lend itself easily to translation (cf. S. de Madariaga, *Englishmen, Frenchmen, Spaniards. An Essay in Comparative Psychology*, London, 1928, pp. 205, 212, 216), and in this respect the *Book of Good Love* is truly Spanish. There exists only one complete English translation, by Elisha Kent Kane, New York, 1933, in the same metrical form. Many stanzas recapture felicitously the musicality and spirited verve of the original, especially in the lyrics; however, quite a few narrative and didactic passages have been marred by Kane's bizarre sense of humor (compare 434d: "los labros de la boca bermejos, angostillos" with the rendition: "The lips that close her little mouth of scarlet must excite The stormy-tender kiss of love, for that is love's delight"; 1509d: "Diz la mora: 'Lesnedri' " [Arab. 'I do not understand'] and "Said she, 'Who is the Sheik?' "), and by his weakness for spicing the text with off-color allusions. Among the fragmentary translations, those by Longfellow are outstanding; yet, in rendering 1678 ff., he adhered less faithfully than did Kane to the original's meters and tone. The already quoted translation of 1606 ff. is far superior, save for the first stanza (see below, n. 22), and for line 1607b: "But little women love so much, one falls in love with sinning," which sounds surprisingly closer to Baudelaire's satanism than to Juan Ruiz's "Es en la dueña chica amor grande e non de poco" [In the little woman there resides great, not small, love].

typical of medieval taste, between a base cover and a noble content, expressed by means of a series of similes (stanzas 16-18). After two devout lyrics to the joys of the Virgin, the "fourfold way" is resumed, once more reminding the reader or listener of the *Book*'s multiple meaning. The admonition to choose the best is concretely imparted in the "Disputation between the Greeks and the Romans," already familiar to you. The poet comments on it at length in very beautiful quatrains, culminating in the last one (70), where the *Book* likens itself to a musical instrument, and warns the reader: "I shall speak to you well or badly according to the talent with which you play on me."

Here is where the autobiographical novel starts. The first adventure is frustrated by the virtue of the lady, and by the intervention of her relatives who slander the poet. It features a variety of fables told by the lady in support of her replies, in the oriental didactic manner, which Juan Ruiz adopts throughout. In this first adventure the courtly tone is distinctly more marked than in the others, and the poet underlines it, assuming here the defense of women.[2] The logical consequence of his defense is that he embarks on a second adventure of a very different tone. Juan Ruiz, enamored this time of a baker woman — by the name of Cross — sends to her his messenger Ferdinand García, who steals her away for himself. After the gay narrative, there follows the lyrical version which, like all other lyrics here, adopts the metric form known in Spanish by the Arabic name of *zéjel;* it is a song formed by a refrain and several stanzas; the last line of each stanza rhymes with the refrain, in which the public doubtless joined the minstrel (115 ff.):

> Eyes, you'll ne'er behold the light
> Since I've lost my Cross tonight.
>
> . . . .
>
> Wanting her within my hand
> I sent García Ferdinand
> Mediator suave and bland
>   To her house at night.
>   [Eyes, you'll ne'er behold the light
>   Since I've lost my Cross tonight.]

[2] To the courtly reasons, Juan Ruiz adds a theological one (stanza 109), also included in the array of arguments with which Chaucer's Dame Prudence buttresses her advice to Melibeus: "Heere may ye see that if that wommen were nat goode, and hir conseils goode and profitable, / oure Lord God of hevene wolde nevere han wroght hem, ne called hem help of man, but rather confusioun of man" (*The Canterbury Tales,* ed. by F. N. Robinson, 2nd ed., Boston, 1957, p. 171b, VII, 1104 f= B², 2294 ff.).

Gladly did he say he'd go;
Secretly he crossed her though —
He ate cake while I ate dough —
　　She was his delight.
[Eyes, you'll ne'er behold the light
Since I've lost my Cross tonight.]

. . . .

Damn that subtle emissary!
Smooth he was, and fast and wary.
May God send him luck contrary
　　For my sorry plight!
[Eyes, you'll ne'er behold the light
Since I've lost my Cross tonight.] [3]

The second defeat provokes new reflections: can man free himself
from the influence of the stars under which he was born? The author,
like so many men of his times, and of many other times, believes
firmly in the power of the stars (a power which he illustrates with the
charming tale of the son of the Moorish King Alcaraz), and he
believes no less firmly in free will and the omnipotence of God, whom
he conceives of as a King capable of breaking the laws that he himself
has laid down. Juan Ruiz was born, of course, under the sign of
Venus, but he does not regret his failures because, he says, love exalts
the one who is in love, thus embroidering upon a thought of Ovid's
repeated by the cultivators of courtly love (156 ff.). All this leads up
to the third adventure, with a perfect lady, who rejects both presents
and songs. And as Sir Love appears to him in a vision, the exasperated Archpriest accuses the god (from the ecclesiastic, and not from
the courtly, viewpoint) of instigating all mortal sins, and he expatiates
on each of them with examples drawn from sacred and classical
history and with fables. Juan Ruiz is an outstanding fabulist, skillful
in breathing drama into the characters, and in bringing to life scenery
and action with lively concrete touches. Many of his best lines are to
be read in his fables and, stranger yet, in the morals appended to
them. Allow me to stop only at the longest fable, titled "Here he
Speaks of the Law-suit which the Wolf and the Fox had Before Sir
Monkey, Judge of the City of Bougie" (321-371). This fable in
Phaedrus' version (I, 10) contains ten lines, and in La Fontaine's (II,
3), seventeen; in the *Book of Good Love* it has grown to two hundred
because, instead of telling that the wolf accuses the fox, the fox denies
the accusation and the monkey condemns the two of them, Juan Ruiz
explains how and why the wolf decided to accuse the fox, and who the

---

[3] Kane's translation, altered in lines 117c and 118b.

lawyers were. He refers to each legal juncture and ramification of the trial, details the involved story of the plaintiffs and the pettifoggers, the manœuvring of the parties and their counsels, and the attempts made to bribe the judge; and he transcribes, so to speak, by means of a parody, the two allegations, the Judge's sentence and its legal justification.[4] Next, Juan Ruiz accuses Sir Love of being the enemy of religion and, continuing the parodical trend, he corroborates his charge with a goliardic description of the daily activities of a cleric in love. The poet points up the correlation between those activities and the divine offices by maliciously applying the corresponding liturgical texts.

Sir Love's answer contains one of the essential elements of the poem, the amorous doctrine which Juan Ruiz completes with rules of morality and urbanity; most of the precepts go back to Ovid's *Art of Love* via a rather sober and bourgeois concept of medieval courtly love. For example, to emphasize the power of gifts, Juan Ruiz inserts another goliardic satire, this time against money, which is said to unsettle society and corrupt the Church (490 ff.) :

> Much power indeed Sir Money has, and much for him we dabble,
> He makes the dolt a man of worth and sets him o'er the rabble,
> He makes the lame leap up and run, he makes the deafmute babble.
> Why, those who have no hands at all will after money scrabble! . . .
> I noticed over there in Rome, where sanctities abound,
> That every one to Money bowed and humbly kissed the ground,
> And paid him many honors with solemnities profound,
> Yes, homaged him upon their knees, as slaves a king surround . . .
> Myself have seen real miracles occur through Money's power,
> As when a man condemned to die is freed within an hour,
> Or when those innocent the gallows presently devour,
> Or when a soul is prayed to Heaven or damned in Hell to cower. . . .[5]

As a practical application of Sir Love's lesson, Juan Ruiz interpolates his paraphrase of the twelfth-century elegiac comedy, *Pamphilus*. Perhaps it is not superfluous to recall that this short Latin work, from whose title our word *pamphlet* is derived, for more than three centuries enjoyed an uncommon success. It was studied in universities, translated into the Romance languages, and imitated in Latin by humanists. Such success is surprising at first sight, because *Pamphilus* cannot compare in artistic achievement with the masterpieces of sentimental literature in the twelfth and thirteenth centuries, the *Énéas*,

---

[4] This fable has been studied as a source of information on legal procedure in Juan Ruiz's time: see M. Eizaga y Gondra, *Un proceso en el "Libro de buen amor,"* Bilbao, 1942.

[5] Kane's translation.

for instance, *Tristan* or the poems of Chrétien de Troyes. Yet, it is not difficult to see where *Pamphilus*' attraction and novelty lie. *Pamphilus* enacts a love whose course is irregular, but which ends at peace with society. This is the theme which has enchanted popular taste from Menander's comedy all the way to the Hollywood films; and *Pamphilus* structures it in a simple plot, rooted in contemporary reality, and reflecting its situations and sentiments under the respected garb of Latin speech and Ovidian motifs. Juan Ruiz, like Fernando de Rojas at a later time, intuitively grasped this incipient realism, and intensified it. Viewed in this perspective, *Pamphilus,* the present episode of the *Book of Good Love,* and *The Celestina* are progressively superior realizations of the same artistic ideal. This situation also entails the proportionately increasing size of the three works. The paraphrase by Juan Ruiz almost doubles the original while hardly altering the plot. This is accomplished not so much by a couple of fables wedged in the dialogue, as by the evocation of a reality distinctly more minute in both its spiritual and material aspects. A single example will suffice; after eliciting some new advice from Lady Venus,[6] the lover goes to speak to his ravishing neighbor — the maiden Galatea in the Latin comedy, the young widow Lady Sloe in the Spanish version — and he describes her first, as he sees her walking down the street. Says Pamphilus (v. 153) :

Oh Lord, how lovely she comes with her uncovered hair!

Sir Melon exclaims (653) :

Oh Lord, how lovely Lady Sloe looks walking through the square!
What swanlike neck and girlish waist, what grace beyond compare,
What little mouth, what color fresh, and what outshining hair,
Though mortally her beaming eyes shoot missiles everywhere!

[6] *Pamphilus* is 780 lines long; its paraphrase in the *Book of Good Love,* 580-891, numbers 311 stanzas, i.e., 1244 lines, but as there are three long lacunae (between stanzas 765-766, 781-782, 877-878: see Ducamin's edition, pp. 136, 138, 154), totaling seventy stanzas, i.e., 280 lines, it actually comprises 1524 lines. Pamphilus' first step is to address Venus, who provides him with pertinent instructions. These instructions closely resemble those Sir Love has already imparted, as both share the same ultimate source, namely, the *Art of Love,* and Juan Ruiz is quite aware of the repetition, since his Lady Venus starts by quoting her "husband" Sir Love's earlier advice (608a). Critics eager to discover in the *Book* the close-knit structure of modern narrative have been at a loss to explain such an obvious case of *double emploi.* As a matter of fact, repetition is inherent in the structure of these Castilian *maqāmāt,* and Juan Ruiz, eager to convey his didactic message, misses no opportunity to hammer home his advice, and to dwell upon the benefits of continuous effort and patient apprenticeship.

The best we can do, then, is to let Sir Melon speak (654 ff.) :

But that was not the sort of place to hold a lover's talk
And, worst of all, a trembling fear did then my pleasure balk,
Till I could neither raise my hands nor use my feet to walk,
But lost my strength, my senses all, and grew as pale as chalk.

I had composed a little speech I thought to say to her,
But bashful fear of passers-by made all my memory blur,
So that I scarcely knew myself nor wot which way to stir,
And then, alas, I found my will and words would not concur . . .

However, this I said to her, "Dear Lady Sloe, my niece
Sends from Toledo, where she lives, her greetings without cease,
And begs, should time and place agree, that you would give her lease
To come to see your grace and thus good fellowship increase. . . ."

I lowered then my voice and said, "I spoke only in jest
Because so many in the square about us closely pressed,"
But when I saw that all were gone and not a soul did rest,
I straight began to talk of love, and thus the lady addressed: . . .

"There's nothing else in all the world I love so much as you;
Two years I have suffered since you came in my unhappy view;
I love you more than I love God, yes, God and all his crew,
But none there is whom I dare trust to go between us two. . . .

My lady, I am sore afraid to tell you more about
My love, until I hear your answer to my prayer devout.
Come, let me know your will in this, and may our hearts speak out!"
Said she, "These words of yours, I hold them less than dregs and grout.

Why, many Lady Sloes that way have been seduced by men,
For men are tricky and deceive the women of their ken.
Don't think that I am such a fool as to believe you when
You patter thus — seek some one else to lure into your den!"

I answered, "Now, my pretty one, how angrily you sport,
As if all fingers were the same — lo, some are long, some short;
As if all men in word and deed were of the same report. . . .

Let not another's naughtiness my innocence mismark,
But come, and let me more explain beneath yon archway dark,
As I would not have all behold us in the open park;
There I may speak in private, here the world's wide ears will hark."

Then, step by step, she softly came beneath the dim, arched hall,
Surpassing beautiful and proud, yet wondrous sweet withal;
Upon a bench of stone she sat and let her lashes fall,
While I once more began what I had hoped her heart would thrall.[7]

After the interview, in which Lady Sloe shows herself courteous but unmoved, Sir Melon, in obedience to the precepts of Sir Love and Lady Venus (based, naturally, on the mores of the period), looks for a go-between. He has the good fortune to run into the unequalled Dame Convent-trotter, whom the author characterizes by developing the few hints of his Latin model. Dame Convent-trotter, attired as a

[7] Kane's translation slightly modified in lines 653ad, 654d, 664d, 669c.

peddler woman, proffers her wares on the street of Lady Sloe, who on hearing her, calls her in. Once she has aroused the young woman's curiosity, Dame Convent-trotter skillfully broaches the subject, pretending to sympathize with Lady Sloe's seclusion (725-727):

> "My child, why do they coop you here?" again began the crone,
> "You will grow old and ugly living by yourself alone,
> Go where your beauty, so acclaimed, will set you in a throne;
> 'Twill not avail you here, within these sullen walls of stone.
> Now in this very town of ours there dwells a pleasant crowd
> Of handsome and attractive youths, most gallant, gay and proud;
> So virtuous in manners that they seem by God endowed;
> Nobody ever saw such men — a fact by all avowed.
> They all have been so kind to me, and on my want took pity,
> But best of all in noble birth, and most exceeding pretty,
> Sir Melon of the Garden is, and furthermore most witty,
> Indeed, in beauty, virtue, grace, he leads our little city."[8]

In the delightful scene which follows, and which is exclusively due to the Archpriest, the pretty widow is too wise to turn her nose up at the possibility of a new marriage; she asks (737):

> "Who is this man, good woman, that you commend so well?
> How much is he worth? Truly, I might consider what you tell."

But when she identifies him with the suitor who spoke to her in the street, she becomes distrustful and alleges more serious worries (742):

> "Stop your solicitations for I've other cares to face;
> Some men have robbed my property and trespassed on my place. . . ."[9]

Here, in a new felicitous characterization, Juan Ruiz shows how Dame Convent-trotter turns to advantage this unforeseen juncture. With a typically Spanish talent for improvisation, she increases the fears of the afflicted widow and introduces Sir Melon as the ideal protector, attributing to him an unsuspected acquaintance with legal matters (743, 755):

> "Now by my faith!" the crone rejoined, "no wonder you are harried
> Worse than a cow; it's all because men see you are not married,
> And therefore take advantages a husband might have parried;
> You'd better get this man before you find too long you've tarried. . . .
> Sir Melon would protect you from their countless suits and cheats
> Because he has been educated in the law's deceits;
> He will defend and run to help whoever him entreats;
> No man can guard you as he can or work such mighty feats."[10]

But Lady Sloe vacillates: the required year of mourning has not yet passed and, if she marries before, she is bound to lose her honor and

---

[8] Kane's translation.
[9] Kane's translation.
[10] Kane's translation.

the inheritance of her first husband. Dame Convent-trotter is too crafty to reply with reasoning; what she does is to wield with much verve and eloquence her argument *ad feminam* (762a):

"What profit is it now to wear those ugly weeds of black? . . ."

Lady Sloe's refusal emphasizes Juan Ruiz's psychological mastery both through what she says and what she leaves unsaid (764):

But Lady Sloe made answer then, "Be silent! I'd not dare
To do what you and he would have — you really must forbear.
Don't press me anymore today with your cajoling prayer,
Nor ask so much and all at once in this unlooked affair. . . ."[11]

In the second interview with Sir Melon, Dame Convent-trotter, out of obedience to a request of Lady Sloe's, puts the lover's sincerity to the test, announcing to him that his lady is going to marry another. Sir Melon goes to such troubadouresque extremes, dolefully berating his heart, his eyes and his tongue, that the old woman, satisfied, consoles him, confiding to him that Lady Sloe is in love, and describing her symptoms: when alone, the two speak always and exclusively of Sir Melon; when someone comes, they change the conversation; the young woman alternately blushes and blanches, her lips quiver, her heart jumps, and she sighs on hearing the name of her beloved. Allow me to observe, at the risk of interrupting the thread of the tale, first, that although the theme of the love signs is not original with the Archpriest, his psychological and stylistic elaboration of it *is* original, particularly the exquisite and, alas, untranslatable handling of the diminutive. Secondly, Lady Sloe has shown no such symptoms of love in the previously narrated interview. That is, Juan Ruiz suggests with expert vagueness scenes which actually are not displayed before the reader, but which make the go-between's persuasion and the change effected in the young woman doubly credible. We shall see that Fernando de Rojas did not fail to grasp such a flexible projection of time and action.

The second interview with Lady Sloe opens with a minor change of circumstances, which demonstrates Juan Ruiz's loathing of the conventional function of lucky coincidence in his model. For in *Pamphilus,* the maid Galatea, supposedly well guarded by her parents, in fact, by "lucky coincidence" is placed into the hands of the procuress whenever she and the author require it. Juan Ruiz has carefully motivated the first entrance of Dame Convent-trotter; on the second occasion, the old woman very naturally runs into Lady Sloe's mother, of whom she must get rid by an improvised lie — which, incidentally,

[11] Kane's translation for stanzas 762a and 764a-d.

does credit to her talents. In the second interview, the Spanish poet decidedly improves upon the Latin in depicting the painful struggle of his heroine between love and honor; but he lacks the skill to trace the complete path of her passion up to the point of her voluntary surrender, as Fernando de Rojas later traces it. And he resolves the difficulty, following in the tracks of his model, that is, through deceit and violence. Old Convent-trotter deceives Lady Sloe into coming to her house where she has stationed Sir Melon; and she leaves the two alone under the pretext of hurrying to answer a neighbor's call.[12] Upon her return, she finds the young woman in tears. With another original psychological touch, the go-between now rejects the reproaches of her victim with almost cynical callousness (878):

> "You claim you knew it was a trick, why then when I went out
> Did you stay with him here alone? Could you not run or shout?
> Don't cast the blame for this on me; you did it, there's no doubt,
> And now the thing to do is not to noise your guilt about. . . ."[13]

But, confronted by the young woman's desperation, she finally proposes marriage; all ends in peace and rejoicing — and seventy-two lines of moralization to caution the ladies in the audience *not* to imitate Lady Sloe's conduct.

There follow new amorous adventures, a quarrel with Dame Convent-trotter in which, with a verbal display worthy of Rabelais, Juan Ruiz enumerates forty-one nicknames which the go-between should not be called, and placates her by ironically conferring upon her the title of his *Book,* namely "Good Love." Then, under cover of Saint Paul's very same precept which heads the autobiographical novel (76cd), the poet narrates his encounters with four cowgirls in the Sierra de Guadarrama, adding at the end of each narrative the corresponding lyrical version, a burlesque pastourelle. As a poet of the city, not of the court, Juan Ruiz is disinclined to idealize country life; his cowgirls are mercenary and lascivious, far more robust and aggressive than the traveler. One exhibits a Goyesque ugliness; the other is a slow-witted lass very much disposed to marrying the poet, who cleverly dodges her under the pretext of going to buy her wedding

[12] The text being defective (see above, n. 6), I summarize the narrative according to *Pamphilus,* vv. 669 ff. As this lacuna corresponds to a lewd scene in the Latin comedy, it has been inferred that the stanzas between 877 and 878 were suppressed because of moral scruples. Yet, some other licentious stanzas have been preserved, and the two other missing passages in the same episode were, so it seems, wholly inoffensive. For an early reader's indignant commentary on Pasiphae's story in the Alfonsine *General estoria,* Part II, see edition by A. G. Solalinde, L. A. Kasten, V. R. B. Oelschläger, Madrid, 1957, Vol. I, p. 396b; the MSS, however, show no trace of mutilation.

[13] Kane's translation.

gifts. In the corresponding pastourelle, the enumeration of rustic tasks and paraphernalia doubtless provoked the laughter of a city audience (997-1005). After extolling worldly love in the mountains, Juan Ruiz pays homage to divine love in the valley, saying his prayers at the sanctuary of Saint Mary of the Vado and composing three pious songs to the Virgin and to Jesus' Passion.

Next comes another long episode of traditional, not autobiographical content, "On the Fight which Sir Carnal Had with Lady Lent."[14] The episode begins with the parodic letters in which Lady Lent challenges Sir Carnal and addresses the faithful. Sir Carnal recruits a numerous host, that is, a group of live animals presented in the order in which their respective kinds of meat appeared at a medieval feast, and each armed with pieces of kitchenware. For example (1086 ff.), in the rearguard of the army go pheasants and peacocks with helmets (which are copper kettles) and shields (which are pots and pans). While Sir Carnal and his retinue sleep after a magnificent banquet, Lady Lent stealthily penetrates into the armed camp and joins the battle. Instead of a second catalogue of foods, the Lenten victuals are woven into the action and are accompanied by their place of origin, so that they constitute a veritable map of Spanish fish and seafood. Inevitably, Lady Lent's troop routs the forces of Sir Carnal, who is taken prisoner. A priest preaches to Sir Carnal and confesses him (here the poet discourses very seriously on "how a Sinner Should Confess, and on Who Has the Power to Absolve Him"), imposing upon him, by way of penance, a mortifying diet. However, on Palm Sunday, while Lady Lent is busy with pious works, Sir Carnal outwits the vigilance of his guardian, Sir Fast, and takes refuge with the Jews, who observe no Lent. Riding on the horse that the rabbi furnishes him, Sir Carnal traverses the cattle-raising region of Spain to the great horror of the herds of livestock, and at the same time, he sends from there a challenge to his rival. But the weeks of Lent are passed, and the "Lady," no longer disposed to sustain the challenge, flees in the guise of a pilgrim (as did the hero of the *Roman de Renard*).

[14] The alternation of seasonal abundance and dearth, many scholars believe, has been a leading impulse for primitive religion and for Greek drama. In the Middle Ages, it inspired debates, parodic poems and rhetorical prose (see Lecoy, *Recherches*, pp. 245 ff.). At the very end of the fifteenth century, the poet and musician Juan del Encina wrote his rustic *Égloga de Antruejo o Carnestolendas* [Eclogue of Carnival], ending in a song ("villancico") whose music is preserved. From the middle of the following century dates Peter Brueghel the Elder's *Combat between Carnival and Lent*, a painting representing a popular celebration of this subject. For an echo in present-day folklore see J. A. Carrizo, *Antecedentes hispano-medioevales de la poesía tradicional argentina*, Buenos Aires, 1945, p. 517.

And now it is April, the spring month heralding the rebirth of nature. Juan Ruiz celebrates the triumphal entrance of the two emperors, Sir Carnal and Sir Love, elaborating with a very personal vision a long poetic tradition traceable to Ovid. Sir Love is received by the trees and singing birds, musical instruments partially personified, and long processions of all the religious hierarchies and orders, which shower the monarch with attention, jokingly applying to him phrases from the liturgy (*Te Amorem laudamus,* for example). The various social classes fight one another for the honor of playing host to the illustrious visitor, and with this aim in mind each satirizes the other and all poke fun at the nuns (1247-1258). Intent on avoiding factions, Sir Love lodges his musical instruments in the poet's house — a charming bit of self-advertising — and has his sumptuous tent pitched in a meadow. With a brevity uncommon in medieval poetry, the Archpriest details a single motif of the decoration of the tent — the allegory of the months; and he discards the customary static description of allegorical figures, in favor of a dynamic evocation of the chores pertaining to each month. At the request of his host, Sir Love tells of his wanderings through Spain, his success and joy in gay Andalusia and his disappointment in austere Castile; of course Juan Ruiz is a Castilian writing for Castilians.

The poet, taking up the thread of his supposed autobiography, once more solicits the offices of Dame Convent-trotter. After two brief unsuccessful adventures, she recommends that he court nuns, who, in addition to preparing titbits and electuaries, surpass all women in charm and courtesy (1332 ff.). Convent-trotter then goes to visit a nun whom she has served before. The nun bears no Christian name; she is called Lady Garoza, which in Arabic means 'bride.' As in the case of Lady Sloe and Dame Convent-trotter, the meaningful name encloses the moral essence of the character. Under the cover of an infidel, Arabic name — the poet seems to insinuate — there is hidden the faithful bride of the Lord. Dame Convent-trotter and Lady Sloe are particular instances of the archetypes which gave birth to them (the procuress, the lady); on the other hand, Lady Garoza acquires her individual existence, belying the type of nun anticipated, in a zigzagging line of constant surprises. The old woman and Lady Garoza debate for two days the pros and cons of worldly love, but the nun, though friendly to her old servant and fond of showing her wit, especially in telling delightful fables, holds her own. Only after hearing the Archpriest's verbal portrait she condescends to speak to him. The go-between leaves on a note of hope, and the poet piles up verses which create the impression that the preventions and delays will only enhance "the good fulfillment" (1498d) of the affair. The rendezvous starts with a line which, in view of the following ones, looks sacrilegious (1499 ff.):

> So in the name of God, next morn, I went to mass right there,
> And lo, I saw the lady kneeling, beautiful, in prayer;
> Her swanlike neck was slim, her color rosy and fair —
> Whoever made her put on sackcloth did her wrong, I swear.
> So help me, Holy Virgin, but I raise my hands, alack,
> Who gave a rose as white as she that ugly habit black? . . .
> She gazed on me with eyes that shone like candles bright,
> "There she is" sighed my heart, and rushed on towards her sight;
> She spoke to me and I to her, in love we took delight.[15]

But a sudden upset saves the initial line, which is not at all sacrilegious: Lady Garoza, the bride of the Lord, is faithful to her vows, and the "good fulfillment" announced is the "clean and chastened love," actually contracted in the name of God (1503 ff.):

> Still she received me only as her loved retainer true,
> And always loyally I did whate'er she'd have me do,
> With clean and chastened love my spirit close to God she drew,
> So that as long as she still lived, that God I loved and knew.[16]

Ultimately, virtuous Lady Garoza is opposed to average nuns, whose weaknesses are denounced, in ironic counterpoint with the initial panegyric (1505). The surprise element[17] is produced all along the episode by the clash between the general category and the particular character who belies it. This curious relationship survives in *The Celestina* and functions there as one of the most delicate devices in the delineation of character. The stanzas describing the beautiful Lady Garoza are apparently akin to a certain type of medieval song which records a nun's complaint against convent life, her curses on

---

[15] Kane's translation, modified in stanzas 1499ac and 1502abc.

[16] Kane's translation.

[17] Playful surprise is a favorite effect with Juan Ruiz, who often tricks the reader into thinking along certain lines, only to bewilder him later by a sudden change of direction. Thus, after repeated admonitions to heed the profound meaning of the poem in order to do it justice, the reader is led to expect that line 64d, which begins: "Understand rightly my *Book*," will be concluded with the remark: "and you will realize it is rightly written" (or some such words), but what he finds instead is the unexpected joke, "and you will get a comely lady." A more sophisticated example occurs in 109 ff., where after praising women in courtly terms, the Archpriest narrates his adventure with the baker-woman, the lowest among the adventures located in city surroundings. Other cases (the lamentation for Convent-trotter, the praise of little women, Sir Ferret's portrait) are dealt with in the following pages; Lady Garoza's story is the longest and most elaborate instance of this zigzagging structure pervading the entire *Book*.

those who immured her, and her yearning for worldly pleasures.[18]
Juan Ruiz has preserved this triple note but has introduced two
fundamental changes. The tone of the nun's complaint is usually
more mocking than sentimental, at times, frankly libertine; Juan
Ruiz's tone is deeply passionate:

Who gave a rose as white as she that ugly habit black?

Moreover, Juan Ruiz avoids showing a nun without vocation, a
lamentable creature, who fails to measure up to the role which destiny
had in store for her. He rather voices in his own name, as a spectator,
the spontaneous pity toward the handsome woman who has renounced
the world. Thanks to these two changes, he extols the merit of the
nun, whom he leaves undefiled on her pedestal of perfection.

But Lady Garoza dies after two months. In the brief adventure
which follows, "How Dame Convent-trotter Spoke to a Mooress on
Behalf of the Archpriest, and the Reply She Gave Her" (1508-1512),
Juan Ruiz, cutting himself loose from all previous known literary
precedents, takes from his daily environment a sliver of life and
elaborates it in the form of a short debate. Here the static nature
of the debate agrees fundamentally with the stubborn opposition of
the Moorish girl to the solicitations of the Christian world. With sly
chatter, Convent-trotter lavishes friendly names on the girl, pretends
sorrow at the long spell passed without seeing her, and joy at her good
fortune. She praises the suitor's gifts, and tries to gain her confidence
by using Arabicized words and idioms. The Moorish girl arrests this
varied game with four laconic replies in her own language — *lesnedrí*
'I don't know,' *legualá* 'no, by Allah,' *ascut* 'be quiet,' *amxí* 'go away.'
All are strategically placed at the end of each stanza, like sonorous
chords which mark her impregnable will. The brief episode of the
Moorish girl contrasts artfully in content, structure and length with
the long episode of the nun and is, unless I am mistaken, the only one
untrammeled by moralization in the entire *Book,* though it has a
moral of its own. The concluding line of the introductory quatrain
superbly sets off the silent and irreproachable girl against her verbose
and sinful lover (1508d):

Her head was full of sense while mine was full of verses.[19]

[18] For further information on the Nun's complaint, see "Nuevas notas para
la interpretación del *Libro de buen amor,*" *NRFH,* XIII (1959), 65 ff. To
the examples and parallels there quoted, add Alfonso de Valdés, *Diálogo de
Mercurio y Carón,* ed. J. F. Montesinos, Madrid, 1929, pp. 94 ff., 225.
[19] Kane's translation. For an interpretation and commentary of the Arabic
words, see J. Oliver Asín, "La expresión *ala ud* en el *Libro de buen amor,*"
Al-Andalus, XXI (1956), 212-214.

The contrast between the appearance of the nun, equivocal to the end, and the unequivocal attitude of the Moorish girl from the beginning, seems hardly accidental. This contradistinction is reflected also in the fondness of the former for displaying her beautiful speech, as compared with the four bare phrases of the Moorish girl, whose exotic language points up her aloofness. The dainty figure of Lady Garoza, at once frivolous and virtuous, emerges slowly from the preliminaries of her episode, from her varied responses throughout the long debate, from the reactions of the old woman and of the lover, and from the surprise element in the zigzagging structure of the episode. The forceful figure of the Moorish girl stands out at once from her four refusals, which undo the plot of the astute go-between. I believe that the unique choice of a Mooress as the heroine of the most effective impersonation of the chaste beloved can only be explained as a deliberate idealization of the Moslem world. The same sentiment prompts other Castilian authors of the fourteenth century to evoke the pomp and sophistication of the Hispano-Arabic courts, thus initiating the nostalgic idealization of the defeated enemy.[20]

In a break in the narration, Juan Ruiz keeps us abreast of his activities as a lyric poet and he enumerates the instruments unsuitable for the accompaniment of Arabic songs. Then he announces the death of Dame Convent-trotter. Under this pretext, "the Archpriest Makes his Lamentation for Her," a sample of a medieval genre in which Spanish poetry has several times achieved rare excellence. Suffice it to recall Jorge Manrique's *Stanzas on the Death of his Father*, as well as the *Lament for Ignacio Sánchez Mejías* by Federico García Lorca. Though the subject is, of course, universal, and the features of its development had been fixed by convention, Juan Ruiz achieves high originality. His guiding sentiment is a deep horror of death, not mitigated by any theological or moral consideration, and it only gives way to what, in fact, is but another facet of the same feeling: the exaltation caused by Jesus' triumph over Death. After the passionate earnestness of these stanzas (1520-1564), the poet, in a characteristic volte-face, mockingly rhapsodizes on old Convent-trotter's sojourn in Paradise, and affixes her epitaph — duly contrite, save for a last naughty line (1578b).

The death of Convent-trotter brings home the capital sins and the

---

[20] See D. Bodmer, *Die granadinischen Romanzen in der europäischen Literatur. Untersuchungen und Texte*, Zurich, 1955; M. S. Carrasco Urgoiti, *El moro de Granada en la literatura (del siglo XV al XX)*, Madrid, 1956, and its critique in *Hispanic Review*, XXVIII (1960), 350-358.

three enemies of man, the Devil, the World, and the Flesh; the moral defense against them proceeds along the lines of the so-called *lorica* theme, in which each virtue is symbolized by a different part of the knightly armor — a theme which had its point of departure in the Bible and was a favorite of medieval piety, because it pictured the righteous man as God's warrior.[21] The line following this ascetic dissertation (1606a), "I wish to make my sermon brief," is a formula to which Juan Ruiz has resorted with some frequency. Here, however, the term "to make brief" ushers in a new section: "Concerning the Qualities which Little Women have," a section still disguised as a simple illustration in the three lines which follow. This is one more example of Juan Ruiz's taste for the zigzagging structure used to obtain a humorous effect. Predisposed by the previous sermon, the reader believes that he stands before another edifying lesson: with a rapid change of direction, the poet embarks on the delightful eulogy which he concludes by paraphrasing the initial words. But precisely upon his return to the starting point, when he would appear to confirm the eulogy, he launches the facetious syllogism which shows how everything was meant from the start to prepare this comic anticlimax (1606 ff.).

> I wish to make my sermon brief, to shorten my oration,
> To a short and concise sermon goes all my approbation,
> — And to a little woman —, and to crisp argumentation
> For few words, cleverly said, get hold of our attention. . . .
> In a little precious stone, what splendor meets the eyes!
> In a little lump of sugar how much of sweetness lies!
> So in a little woman love grows and multiplies,
> You recollect the proverb says, — a word unto the wise. . . .
> And as within the little rose you find the richest dies,
> And in a little grain of gold much price and value lies,
> As from a little balsam much odor doth arise,
> So in a little woman there's a taste of paradise.
> Even as the little ruby its secret worth betrays,
> — Color, and price, and virtue, — in the clearness of its rays,
> Just so a little woman much excellence displays,
> Beauty, and grace, and love, and fidelity always.
> The skylark and the nightingale, though small and light of wing,
> Yet warble sweeter in the grove than all the birds that sing,
> And so a little woman, though a very little thing,
> Is sweeter far than sugar, and flowers that bloom in spring. . . .

[21] See Lecoy, *Recherches,* pp. 184 ff., and *The Oxford Book of Medieval Latin Verse,* ed. S. Gaselee, Oxford, 1928, n. 26 and note on p. 212; add Saint Cyprian, *Epistle LVIII,* ix, 1.

> If as her size increases are woman's charms decreased,
> Then surely it is good to be from all the great released,
> Now of two evils choose the less, — said a wise man of the East,
> By consequence, of woman-kind be sure to choose the least.[22]

The last adventure of the *Book,* like one of the first, miscarries through a messenger's fault. It contains the moral portrait of the poet's messenger, ironically dubbed Sir Ferret,

> an exceeding genteel lad,
> Except for fourteen blemishes, a better one I never had.

The portrait consists of an accumulation of defects ("A trouble-making liar he was, and a drunkard and a thief. . . ."), in that humorous pattern found likewise, as we have seen, in the *Book of Delights* of Yosef ben Meir ibn Zabarra and in a host of subsequent humorists.

The version of 1343 adds, besides, an episode concerning the commotion in Talavera occasioned by Pope Benedict XII's letter to the Spanish ecclesiastical authorities, admonishing them to tighten clerical discipline. The papal efforts in this direction had given rise during the previous century — and, apparently, in England — to various brilliant goliardic satires which lashed at the resistance of the lower clergy to the severe precepts of their superiors. The Archpriest, with his masterly use of concrete touches, and his splendid gift for making the characters speak in direct discourse, dramatically casts a piece of contemporary reality into an inherited mold.[23]

The *Book* concludes with careful symmetry: the "Joys of Saint Mary" at the beginning are echoed by new devout songs to the Virgin, among others, the gem of Juan Ruiz's religious lyric (1678-1683):

> I would that I might follow Thee, Thou flower among the flowers,
> I would that I in praise of Thee might ever fill the hours,
> Nor would I swerve
> If I could serve
> The best which all my best embowers.
> I pour my confidence in Thee, mine heart entire I pour,

[22] Longfellow's translation, except for lines 1606bcd, which read: "For a never ending sermon is my utter detestation; I like short women, — suits at law without procrastination, And am always most delighted with things of short duration." Compare the Spanish: "Ca siempre me pagué de pequeño sermón / e de dueña pequeña e de breve razón, / ca lo poco e bien dicho finca en el coraçón." For further information on the saying "the smaller woman is the better," see "Nuevas notas," pp. 26 f. Add Angelo Poliziano's *Tagebuch,* ed. A. Wesselski, Jena, 1929, No. 145.

[23] See Menéndez Pidal's brilliant study of this episode in *Poesía juglaresca,* pp. 205 ff.

For Thou, my Lady, art mine hope and life for evermore.
From sorrow's sway
Without delay
Come, free me, Virgin, I implore. . . .
Here innocent I suffer wrong, in woe I make my bed,
And know that yet a little while and I'll be with the dead;
Oh succor me
For none I see
To free me from this awful dread.[24]

There are a few more songs — of blind men, of mendicant students, to Chance — by way of an appendage of separate compositions. The true conclusion of the *Book,* matching the long introduction (44 ff.), is the Epilogue entitled "How the Archpriest Says this Book of His Should be Understood." In it, Juan Ruiz once more dwells upon the title, the content, and the correct interpretation of his poem, particularly upon its recondite meaning, which will be revealed only through the attentive meditation of future readers. Once more, then, and with almost solemn gravity, Juan Ruiz expounds the curious medieval concept of the book, not as a whole actually given to the passive reader, but as a bare outline (the text), whose potential completion the reader must achieve by virtue of his own active effort (the gloss). The Archpriest takes his leave, apologizing modestly for his performance as a minstrel; and at the same time, asking no longer as a minstrel but as a didactic poet — like Cynewulf or Gonzalo de Berceo — for the spiritual reward of the listener's prayers. To the modern reader, haunted by his notions (in the last analysis, Greco-Roman),[25] of artistic unity and artistic categories, this book remains contradictory to the end. For it is a *mudéjar* book, composed by a Christian priest linked to an Arabic and Judaic tradition, and its vibrant stanzas encompass all the variety of the universe under its title of *Good Love,* "which is the love of God," true Author of everything.

[24] Kane's translation.
[25] G. Williams, *The Burning Tree,* London, 1956, pp. 13 and 15, comments on simultaneous contrary moods and on the absence of a centered design in Welsh poetry, both peculiarities due to its independence of Greco-Roman heritage. Poems 11 and 12 by Hywel ab Owain Gwynedd (twelfth century) provide a significant counterpart of Juan Ruiz's attitude toward Christian devotion and Ovidian lore.

CHAPTER FOUR

The Celestina: The Plot and Its Development

One finds few literary works whose plot is simpler than that of *The Celestina.* Calisto, rejected by Melibea, resorts on the advice of his servant Sempronio to the procuress Celestina; she obtains Melibea's assent and a rich reward from Calisto. Sempronio and another servant quarrel with Celestina for their share of the payment; they murder her and are punished with death. Calisto, on returning from Melibea's arms, trips on the ladder and falls to his death. Melibea throws herself from her tower. Thus goes the older version; in the 1502 version, lengthened at the request of the readers, Calisto and Melibea die but not immediately after the first night of love. Elicia and Areúsa, Celestina's protégées and the dead servants' paramours, send some ruffians to avenge them. Calisto, on a new rendezvous, hears the noise they make, hurries to face them, falls down and dies. That is all. Compared with *Romeo and Juliet* — a play with which the *Tragicomedy* shows notable similarities and fundamental differences — it surprises the reader, on the one hand, by its much greater length — twenty-one acts instead of five — and, on the other, by its much less intricate plot. Moreover, *Romeo and Juliet* packs twenty-five characters, a chorus, throngs of citizens, members of the Montague and Capulet families, maskers, guards, watchmen, and attendants. *The Celestina* is bare of chorus and retinues, and the characters (one of whom, Crito, utters just four words) are thirteen in the older and fourteen in the definitive version. In *Romeo and Juliet,* no less important than love is the hostile pressure of the outside world, personified in the factions of Verona, a pressure which turns out to surpass love in power. The basic outline of *The Celestina* is more elemental and more pessimistic: even without the intrusion of external forces, it shows love smashed in its own course. What meaning, then, shall we assign to the unusual simplicity of the plot and the unusual proportions of its development?

A glance at the literary tradition to which *The Celestina* pertains may, I believe, aid us in understanding it. Rojas himself, in a preliminary stanza, characterizes Act I as a "Terentian work," and one of its earliest imitators declares that "any dialogue is cast in Terence's style."[1] Indeed, the examination of *The Celestina* shows that Roman and especially Terentian comedy was the model, direct and indirect, for a good number of technical devices; it has fixed the categories of most characters (the lovers, the parents, the servants, the courtesans) ; it has imposed the love theme, and has left a tangible trace in some situations and in innumerable maxims and verbal echoes. At the same time, the analysis of *The Celestina* also bares very marked divergencies, which stand out if one compares it with the Italian *commedia erudita,* initiated by Ariosto and Machiavelli, or with Molière's comedy, which both conform distinctly more to the Roman norm. *The Celestina* discards many unrealistic technical artifices of the Roman comedy, re-works with great independence even those which it does adopt, and above all, imitates Terence in the purely formal, external aspects, but in neither the subject matter nor the emotional tone, still less in the environment and the characters. In one thousand lines, the average length of a Roman comedy, there is hardly space to sketch more than types and caricatures, and to suggest vaguely the conventional Greek background inherited from its originals. As for the difference in subject matter and emotional tone, suffice it to recall that in most Roman comedies, the young master, in order to carry a love affair with a courtesan or with a girl of supposedly humble birth, needs money. His slave, invariably faithful and cunning, secures it through his ability to take advantage of the wicked slavedealer, who owns the courtesan, or of the young man's stern father. Thus, the tricks used to succeed in a mercenary intrigue are of more concern than love itself.[2] In *The Celestina,* though Calisto fulfills his love with the help of people of low station, there are no tricks; the nucleus of the play consists in the love of the protagonists, and in the interests and passions which this feeling unleashes.

[1] Pedro Manuel Jiménez de Urrea, *Penitencia de amor* (ed. R. Foulché-Delbosc, Barcelona-Madrid, 1902, p. 3): "y naturalmente es estilo del Terencio lo que hablan en ayuntamiento."

[2] Plautus piles up obstacles the more to enhance the ingenuity of the *seruus fallax:* see, for instance, the comedies *Bacchides,* vv. 739 ff. and *Pseudolus,* vv. 508 ff., where the trickster draws out the money from the *durus pater* though he himself, for virtuosity's sake, has forewarned the old man to be on his guard. Once the intrigue has been successfully carried out, Plautus sometimes does not so much as condescend to enact the dénouement, and he reports it in a few hurried lines (*Casina,* vv. 1012 ff.; cf. *Cistellaria,* vv. 774 ff.). Terence resorts to his typical procedure of *contaminatio* mainly to heighten the artful sophistication of the intrigue. Both Plautus and Terence introduce in their comedies slaves revelling in admiration at their own scheming abilities (*Bacchides,* vv. 640 ff., 925 ff.; *Miles gloriosus,* v. 813; *Pseudolus,* vv. 575 ff.; *Heauton timorumenos,* vv. 709 ff.).

Apropos of the episode of Lady Sloe in the *Book of Good Love* and
its source, *Pamphilus,* we became acquainted with elegiac comedies.
They are brief plays, in Latin elegiac distichs, usually of scant merit,
composed in the main between the twelfth and the thirteenth centuries, principally in France and Italy. On the whole, apart from the
use of some names, turns and phrases, they owe much more to Ovid's
love poems than to Roman comedy. The plots are simple; background scenery is confined to a minimum; however, it draws not on
the ancient but on contemporary environment: Pamphilus and
Galatea dwell in a medieval city; Galatea is alone because her parents
have gone to mass, etc. In like fashion, these plays have altered the
categories of personages which Roman comedy featured; for instance,
a new figure appears, the go-between hired by the lover. Moreover,
the presentation of the protagonists and of their servants is radically
different and echoes the conditions and biases of the period. Furthermore, since the plot no longer centers on schemes contrived by the
servants, the hero is less eclipsed by them. The heroine steps out of the
penumbra in which Greco-Roman comedy kept her, participates
actively in the dialogue and, at times, seizes the initiative. As a result,
the servants' role is rather secondary and, in diametrical opposition to
Roman comedy, they are characterized by selfishness and disloyalty.
In the comedy *Baucis et Traso,*[3] for instance, one of the servants allies
himself with the covetous procuress to exploit his master, just as in
The Celestina. This novel trait reflects the medieval writer's un-
friendly reaction to humble folk. In his uniform malice, the medieval
servant is no less false to reality than was the slave of the ancient
theater in his uniform loyalty and abnegation. But instead of being a
mere tool of the protagonist, the servant has now become an autonomous creature. The importance of this innovation, which *The Celestina* carries to its extreme artistic consequences, is at once visible. As
for the emotional tone, these plays are quite variable, but even though
most are of cheerful intent, they overflow with sentiment. In this
they deviate from Roman comedy and display the eroticism which
pervades so many forms of Latin and vernacular literature, from the
twelfth century onward. Love is consistently illicit, some situations
being singularly obscene; nevertheless, the authors grant it their
sympathy and place at its service all their skill for rhetorical variation.
Precisely *Pamphilus,* which anticipates the outline of *The Celestina,*
stands out through its sentimentalism. The soliloquies and tirades of

---

[3] For this comedy, as well as for *Pamphilus,* see G. Cohen, *La "Comédie"
latine en France au XII*ᵉ *siècle,* II, Paris, 1931.

the protagonists, their attempts at amorous introspection, uncover, underneath the Ovidian adornment, motivations and concepts of the *roman courtois*. This appears in the troubadouresque reproaches of Pamphilus aimed at his heart and senses, upbraidings which have left a lasting imprint on a similar situation in the *Tragicomedy* (VI, 218, 222 f.). *Pamphilus* also offers the first appearance in drama of the heroine who, in emphatic contrast to the easy loves of Plautus and Terence, painfully struggles with herself, like Lavine in the *Énéas* or Soredamor and Phénice in *Cligès*. The agitated monologue of Melibea, who is torn between passion and honor (X, 53 ff.), comes exceedingly close to Galatea's complaint (*Pamphilus*, 573 ff.), both in dramatic context and emotional tone.

In the fourteenth century and, to all appearances, initiated by no less a writer than Petrarch, there emerges in Italy a new dramatic form which flourishes until the first years of the sixteenth century: the humanistic comedy. A few of these plays are written in verse; most are in prose, of quite varied style and quality. The influence of Plautus and Terence is considerable, above all in the later specimens, but external. Humanistic comedy aspires to a rich and free portrayal of reality. As a means to this end, it indiscriminately adopts the devices offered by Roman and elegiac comedy, as well as by the medieval religious theater. At times, this has resulted in a degree of verisimilitude incomparable with that of its antecedents, as in the use of the aside and in the presentation of place and time, which are its principal technical contributions to *The Celestina*. With few exceptions, it resembles elegiac comedy in that the plot remains very simple, the theme is illicit love, and the view of this feeling is the medieval, not the ancient one. Another essential departure from Roman comedy, along with the simplification of the plot, is the very slow pace which allows for expansion of the brief action. The summary of one of the best humanistic comedies, *Poliscena*, attributed to Leonardo Bruni d'Arezzo, states: "This is all there is to the comedy, but the poet enlarges upon it in a marvelous way." Indeed, it must have been marvelous for the readers of Plautus and Terence to find in the new genre a slow motion, so to speak, which delights in the repetition of situations and characters (aiming at delicate shading rather than at sharp contrast), in the abundance of episodes not essential to the action (although very valuable for other purposes), and in the motivation which justifies with inexhaustible detail each turn of the story.

Thanks to this slow motion, all humanistic comedies, even those most attached to the external imitation of Plautus and Terence, are permeated by actual reality, in Italian cities. As for characters, humanistic comedy introduces many copied from contemporary life, and reworks with astonishing lack of convention the inherited categories, above all the relationship between parents and children and, more curious still, between fathers and daughters. The predominant type of the lover is the merely sensual one. But there are on record some original variations, the favorite being the dreamy and ineffectual lover,[4] immortalized in the traits of Calisto. The most radical innovation affects the heroine. As in elegiac comedy the enamored girls explode with vehement passion, and protest against the social conventions which chain their emotions, in terms traceable to the *roman courtois:* both traits culminate in Melibea's passion and protest. The faithful servants in the style of Roman theater outnumber the villains, after the manner of elegiac comedy, but they inherit the latters' autonomous personality and amorous adventures, independent of those of their masters. Thus, the slow motion permits a uniquely important novelty: that of bestowing the same measure of attention and of artistic sympathy to each of the characters, whatever his moral or social status may be.

The humanistic comedy was dislodged in Italy by the advent of the *commedia erudita,* riding the crest of the revival of Greco-Roman Antiquity, but not without leaving most noteworthy vestiges in the vernacular. To begin with, there exist the so-called *drammi mescidati,* structured in harmony with ancient convention — five acts in verse, choruses at the end of the acts — though they retain the representation of place and time as practiced by the medieval theater, offer a variety of subjects and lead to a tragic dénouement. The subjects, preferably amorous, are treated with the deep sympathy inherent in the *roman courtois,* and the ending is tragic. Secondly, the humanistic comedy left in the vernacular one example of great merit, *La Venexiana* [The Venetian Comedy], the work of an unknown author, composed at the dawn of the sixteenth century.[5] It has a very simple

---

[4] See, for instance, Pier Paolo Vergerio, *Paulus,* ed. K. Müllner, *Wiener Studien,* XXI-XXII (1901), 232 ff.; Leon Battista Alberti, *Philodoxus,* ed. A. Bonucci, *Opere volgari,* I, Florence, 1843, pp. cxx ff.; Tito Livio Frulovisi, *Oratoria,* ed. C. W. Previté-Orton, *Opera hactenus inedita,* Cambridge, England, 1932; the anonymous *Aetheria,* ed. E. Franceschini, *Atti e memorie della R. Accademia di Scienze, Lettere ed Arti in Padova,* Nuova Serie, LVI (1939-40), 103 ff.; Johannes de Vallata, *Poliodorus,* ed. J. M. Casas Homs, Madrid, 1953.

[5] For the *drammi mescidati,* see V. Rossi, *Il Quattrocento,* 3rd-4th ed., Milan, 1953, p. 532; I. Sanesi, *La Commedia,* 2d ed., Milan, 1954, pp. 208 ff. *La Venexiana* was published for the first time by E. Lovarini, Bologna,

plot and slow pace and, in addition, gives the impression of being unfinished. In its five acts it displays minutely the characters and motivations of its few personages; without exactly describing or enumerating, it manages to suggest the opulence and activity of Venice. In power of characterization it surpasses all other humanistic comedies. Its six characters are portrayed by their own deeds and words as well as by their manner of describing each other. Their actions are motivated by their own personalities rather than by external impulses. As a whole, the work is anything but lighthearted. A sombre, passionate tone predominates in it, and lurks even in the most risqué scenes. Such scenes are at no point repulsive because they are not mere inserts meant to provoke laughter (as in the *commedia erudita*), but they rigorously obey the general plan. All these traits reappear in *The Celestina*.

Various textual resemblances make it plain that the authors of *The Celestina* were acquainted with some humanistic comedies. On examination, our play shares with most of these the prose form, the techniques of the Roman comedy as well as those contributed by the medieval comedy and, above all, their fluid and impressionistic conception of space and time.[6] Like almost all humanistic comedies, *The Celestina* brings to the stage a simple case of illicit love, accomplished through the mediation of servants and a go-between. Its slow advance motivates the simple plot with great detail, using as a favorite resource the passions and interests of the characters, and thanks to this psychological motivation the action takes on a tragic fatality which the mere interplay of external causes could scarcely have given it.[7] This leisurely pace delights in stressing the ironic incompatibility between the meaning which the characters give to the action and the

1928; cf. Sanesi, *Saggi di critica e storia letteraria,* Milan, 1941, pp. 223 ff.; Benedetto Croce, *Poesia popolare e poesia d'arte,* 2d ed., Bari, 1946, pp. 299 ff.

[6] For contacts between humanistic comedy and *The Celestina,* see M. Menéndez Pelayo, *Orígenes de la novela,* III, Madrid, 1910, pp. lxix ff.; and *Nueva Revista de Filología Hispánica,* X (1956), 415 ff.

[7] Cf. T. S. Eliot, "Wilkie Collins and Dickens" (*Selected Essays,* London, 1932, p. 467): "What is the difference between *The Frozen Deep* [a melodrama by Collins] and *Œdipus the King*? It is the difference between coincidence, set without shame or pretence, and fate — which merges into character. It is not necessary for the high drama that accident should be eliminated; you cannot formulate the proportion of accident that is permissible. But in great drama character is always felt to be — not more important than plot, but somehow integral with plot. At least, one is left with the conviction that if circumstances had not arranged the events to fall out in such and such a way, the personages were, after all, such that they would have ended just as badly, or just as well, and more or less similarly."

meaning it holds for the authors and the readers, and transforms into a systematic procedure the parallelism of characters, utterances and situations, so as to underline the similarity and infinite diversity of reality.

Precisely because the main artistic goal of the *Tragicomedy* is to reflect that complex reality which ties together even the few events of the most elementary drama, rather than to devise an ingenious intrigue entangling the characters from the outside, we find a stringent sequence of causes and effects from the moment in which, as we are informed in the Argument to Act I, "Calisto enters a garden in pursuit of a falcon. He finds Melibea there, and falling in love with her, begins to talk to her." Melibea harshly rejects Calisto's compliments, suspecting a sinful intention in his sacrilegious flattery. In the scene which follows, Calisto calls his servant Sempronio and bids him prepare the bedroom into which he hurries to take refuge. Remember that in Roman and Italian comedy, in that of the Spanish Golden Age, as well as in Molière's, the servant is rarely seen at work, but acts instead as a confidant or accomplice, as a creature of literary convention. *The Celestina,* however, possesses the dramatic distinction (in the genuine meaning of the word "dramatic") of showing the characters in action. The servant appears functioning as a servant, busy with the chores of his job, and abiding by the requisites of his social condition. For this reason, although Calisto's insane demeanor awakens Sempronio's curiosity — above all because it may affect him — he refrains from rashly advising Calisto on his own, but considers which side to take. Hesitating he weighs the solutions his greed and cowardice alternately suggest to him. Only a new call from his master cuts short his doubts; he then preaches the misogyny which he does not practice, and pedantically inveighs against women's frailties. But as Calisto persists, Sempronio in the end seconds him. His weak will and his avidity, stirred by the inducement of a gift — in a word, his own character — prompts him to recommend Celestina.

Sent by Calisto to search for her, he arrives at a rather inopportune moment, when his mistress Elicia is catering to another client, Crito. Luckily, Celestina is there to teach the young woman how to hide Crito, informing him that her cousin has just arrived, and to detain the caller with feigned affection. Once her lover is concealed, Elicia simulates jealousy and grief because Sempronio has let three days pass without coming to visit her. He listens with delight to her insults and endeavors to console her with beautiful passionate phrases, which he interrupts only on hearing the footsteps of Crito, locked in the loft where the brooms are kept. Elicia, toying with danger, puts on a show of being offended, and invites him to go and find out by himself what is happening upstairs. Once again Celestina has to intervene, improvising a lie on the spur of the moment: the footsteps are those of a certain girl reserved for a certain fat priest. Then Sempronio, satisfied, conducts Celestina to Calisto's house. The relaxing scene just outlined is one of the many that exert little influence on the progress of the plot. This one separates the agitated dialogue of love and self-interest between Calisto and Sempronio from the dialogue of conspiracy and calculation between Sempronio and Celestina. It highlights the quick intelligence and the gift for improvisation with which the old woman extricates herself from the most difficult situations and dominates her interlocutors. It also depicts Elicia's nervous irascibility, her treachery and her fondness for deceiving with half-truths. Finally, this scene shows Sempronio, who only a moment ago had put Calisto on guard against the deceits of women, grotesquely outwitted by the procuress and her pupil.

En route to Calisto's house, in a conversation typical of the free representation of movement in this drama, Sempronio tells Celestina of his commission, and underlines the common advantage to be gained. On this point of shared profit, the old woman does not answer, thus insinuating the conflict of avarice that is bound to separate them. When they knock at the door, Calisto sends another servant, Pármeno, to open. Since his mother was an old friend of Celestina's, Pármeno is able to alert his master to the infamy of the old woman, whose disrepute in the city and whose skill in witchcraft and corruption he particularizes with obvious fascination. But his warnings have no effect on Calisto, who is intent upon satisfying his love by whatever means. Celestina overhears Pármeno's hostile words; for this reason, as soon as Calisto returns upstairs, accompanied by Sempronio (to look for the money needed to reward her services), Celestina launches against Pármeno a long offensive, in which she tries out all possible arguments to attract him and thus to whittle away his opposition to her lucrative deal with Calisto. At last she finds his price: the love of one of her girls, Areúsa.

Calisto, after taking leave of the go-between, sends Sempronio off to hurry her, and remains in the company of Pármeno, whose opinion he asks on the agreement with Celestina. Pármeno, who had previously declared himself convinced by her allegations and promises, now face to face with his master, honestly points out again the danger of confiding his secret to such an infamous woman. Celestina's persuasion, strong enough to have broken down his intellectual defenses, has failed to take possession of the deepest levels of his personality. Calisto, who has asked Pármeno's opinion in hopes that it might coincide with his own, becomes irritated on hearing a contrary recommendation, and orders him to saddle his horse so that he may pass by Melibea's house. This order gravely offends Pármeno, who sees his status lowered and himself insulted by such ingratitude. Meanwhile, Sempronio has reached Celestina and acquaints her with his master's haste. She explains the dangers of the undertaking — which terrify Sempronio — and boasts of her ability to overcome them. Returning home, she leaves Sempronio in Elicia's company and, with grand mythological pomp and sumptuous style — Fernando de Rojas' tribute to the literary fashion of his times — she invokes the help of "gloomy Pluto, Lord of the Infernal Regions Subterranean, Emperor of the Court of the Damned," for the enterprise on which she is going to embark.

Magic conjuration notwithstanding, on setting out alone for Melibea's house Celestina's natural terror appears in an anguished soliloquy; for if Melibea's parents find out about her message-bearing, she risks nothing less than her skin. But she deliberately resolves to risk it because, with admirable psychological insight, Rojas shows her placing her professional honor before anything else. At Melibea's door she beholds the servant Lucrecia, a cousin of her protégée Elicia, and succeeds in reaching Melibea and her mother Alisa under the pretext of selling thread. While the sale is being negotiated, a page arrives to call Alisa to the bedside of her sick sister. Here Rojas makes use of a double plane of causality, probably adopted from Greco-Roman epic and tragedy. Alisa's departure surprises Celestina, who fancies seeing in it the intervention of the "gloomy Pluto, Lord of the Infernal Regions" she has invoked, but it causes no surprise to Alisa, Melibea or Lucrecia, for, as is repeatedly implied in the text, the lady pays daily visits to her sick sister. On the other hand, if Alisa, for all her knowledge of Celestina's nature, has no hesitation about leaving her with Melibea, this is due to her blind confidence in her daughter — a tragic mistake, which conditions the plot. There follows a long, involved dialogue, in which with skillful evasions Celestina draws near her purpose and, at the urgent request of Melibea, finally announces that she comes on behalf of a sick person whom Melibea might save "with just one word from her noble lips" — the sick being, of course, Calisto. On hearing the name, the young lady bursts into loud threats and insults. Celestina, with her gift for improvisation, hurries to add that what is afflicting Calisto is a toothache, and that what she comes to solicit in his name is the prayer to Saint Apollonia,[8] and also Melibea's cord, which has touched religious relics of Rome and Jerusalem. The girl can hardly hide her disappointment at learning that this is all. Celestina sees through her, and the conversation about the sick gentleman continues with masterly equivocation. Melibea hands over the cord, for "it is a pious and holy work to heal the suffering and the sick," and adds (IV, 189): "As there is no time to write the prayer down before my mother's return, if the cord is not enough, come back tomorrow for the prayer — very secretly." At which point the servant Lucrecia remarks: "Aha! My mistress is lost. So she wants Celestina to come secretly? There is some trick in this. She will give her more than she has said."

The old woman rushes to Calisto's house complimenting herself on her adroitness. Sempronio is waiting for her and realizes how radically the situation has changed. Celestina is no longer the grateful accomplice in the profitable deal which he has brought her. She is no longer disposed to share her impressions and her reward with him. In the exaltation caused by her triumph, she becomes tight-lipped, so as to keep for herself all of Calisto's gratifications. Finally, she lets a fatal word escape (V, 196): "Though you are to have some small share of the profit. . . ." "Some small share, Celestina?" inquires Sempronio, "I do not like that word of yours." Quick-witted, she tries to cover up her slip: "Hush, silly, a small share or a big share, I shall give you as much as you wish. Everything I have is yours." But the harm has already been wrought: that "small share" is the Sophoclean "little word,"[9] pregnant with tragic consequences, for Sempronio begins to see through the schemes of his formidable ally. This repartee, then, opens the breach which will end with her assassination and his execution.

In the presence of Calisto and the two servants, Celestina relates her interview with Melibea, begging insistently for a cloak and a skirt — a recompense which offers the advantage of lending itself to no sort of partition. The scene is typical of Rojas' deftness in setting off the diverse responses of his characters to a single stimulus. Calisto, engrossed by his amorous pursuit, has eyes and ears only for satisfying it.

[8] Armando Palacio Valdés' novel *El cuarto poder* [The Fourth Estate], Ch. ix, 1888, still bears witness to the popularity of this prayer. For current versions in Spanish and Spanish American folklore, see *Quixote*, Part I, Ch. vii, ed. F. Rodríguez Marín, Madrid, IV, 1916, pp. 153 f.

[9] See especially *Œdipus at Colonus*, vv. 443 and 620; cf. my *Introducción al teatro de Sófocles*, Buenos Aires, 1944, p. 82.

Pármeno, resentful of Calisto's injustice and entirely aware of the old woman's perfidy, comments sarcastically on the actions of both. Sempronio wishes to keep him within bounds, but is torn between the prospects with which Celestina dazzled him, and the despair caused by her increasingly manifest intention of cheating him out of his portion. At last, Calisto, on receiving Melibea's cord, orders Pármeno to have the tailor hand the desired clothes to the go-between. Out of spite, Pármeno observes that it is very late and thus manages to postpone the gift. As it is night, Calisto has Celestina accompanied home by Pármeno. She tries once more to bring him to her way of thinking, shielding herself with the mention of his mother's infamy. To get rid of this enemy, more sharp-witted, hence more dangerous than Sempronio, Celestina leaves reasoning aside and proceeds to deliver Areúsa to him. She goes up to see the girl, who is already in bed, overwhelms her with her flow of words, conquers her fears and indecision, her residue of modesty, and lasciviously flings in her bed the adolescent Pármeno; he, upon seeing the tart, loses all control of himself, and concedes to the old woman whatever she asks of him. With perfect psychological consistency, the moral corruption which she has achieved will soon turn against her.

In the following act, amid raillery and confessions,[10] the two servants seal their friendship, taking advantage of Calisto and draining his wealth. He is so obsessed by his love, with no other consolation than poetry and music, that he fails as much as to notice them. And while he rushes to church to pray devoutly that Mary Magdalene, the patroness of lovers, grant him the grace of seducing Melibea, the two servants indulge in a feast at his expense in Celestina's house in the company of their girls. As a topic of conversation Sempronio proposes "the love affair of this crazy master of ours and of the gracious and lovely Melibea"; but it so happens that the girls disagree with his masculine evaluation. They have no quarrel with Calisto, but find fault in everything that is Melibea's: her beauty, her wealth, her

---

[10] Pármeno's exultant monologue and his search for a confidant (VIII, 8 f.) have their point of departure in Terence, *Eunuchus*, vv. 549 ff.: here the youth Chaerea escapes from the courtesan's house after raping a young girl, and by "lucky coincidence" meets a friend of his, who appears precisely to play the rôle of the confidant, and disappears as soon as the confession is over. Rojas' painstaking motivation is strikingly opposed to such slipshod technique. The pleasure of exchanging love-confidences and Areúsa's possession have been the two temptations Celestina dangled before Pármeno in her first talk to him; the enjoyment of both marks, then, the success of the scheme contrived by the old woman from the outset. At the same time, it marks the starting point of the servants' close alliance, which is to end in Celestina's discomfiture.

lineage, all that she owns and they lack. "If she looks beautiful,"
vociferates the irritable Elicia, "it is because of all the finery she has
on. Put it on a stick: you will also say it is lovely. On my life, and
I don't say this to praise myself, but I think I am as beautiful as your
Melibea." Her cousin Areúsa seconds her, arguing that the beauty of
the high-born lady is, in truth, the result of ill-smelling cosmetics which
hardly cover her senile deformity. And she concludes with a protest
that is no less revealing of the inferiority which oppresses them: "I
cannot imagine what Calisto has seen in her, why he turns away from
the love of other girls he could have more easily, and with whom he
could enjoy himself the more." Celestina restores peace, but at that
moment there is a knock at the door. Lucrecia has come to look for
the old woman; she has been sent by Melibea, who "is fatigued with
swoons and heartache." Despite the urgency of the ailment, the
serving-girl stops a good while to listen to Celestina who, inspired by
remembrance of things past and by the jug which solaces her, recalls
her years of splendor, when no fewer than nine girls between fourteen
and eighteen years old would sit at her table: "Mine the profit, theirs
the toil. And hadn't I compliant friends because of them? Old gentlemen and young, clergymen of all ranks from bishops to sextons. When
I entered a church I saw hats doffed in my honor as if I were a
duchess." But suddenly she comes back to reality, as her ironic com-
ment on Melibea's ailment proves: "I wonder why such a young
woman should have a heartache."

In truth, Melibea, enamored of Calisto since she first set eyes on
him, as she herself confesses, still fights between love and honor, between the sincerest desire to hide her love and the irrepressible yearning to reveal it. In a long scene, at times almost comical, at times
singularly lyrical, which elaborates upon the revelation of love through
the name of the beloved,[11] she finally declares her passion and grants
a rendezvous through closed doors for the following night. On leaving, Celestina unexpectedly runs into Alisa, who is returning home —

[11] In Western literature, such revelation has been traditional since Euripides,
Hippolytus, vv. 304 ff., 345 ff.; cf. Ovid, *Metamorphoses,* X, 401 ff.; *Énéas,*
vv. 1275 ff., 1324; Gautier d'Arras, *Éracle,* vv. 4199 ff. However, the differences between *The Celestina* and this tradition are highly indicative of Rojas'
realistic art of motivation. In the Greek, Latin, and French instances, an old
woman, out of sincere affection, questions the lover, whose ailment she rightly
diagnoses, and by "lucky coincidence" hits upon the name of the beloved.
Rojas neither shares such optimistic faith in "lucky coincidence," nor believes
that humble people serve the high-born out of pure affection. Celestina
arrives because Melibea has sent for her; she need not interpret the "patient's"
symptoms because she well knows what ails her; she pronounces Calisto's
name not by chance, but deliberately, so as to elicit Melibea's confession.

doubtless from the daily visit to her sick sister — and Alisa asks distrustfully why she has come. "To bring some thread that was missing yesterday," improvises the go-between. Alisa next interrogates her daughter, who answers with another lie, foreseeably a different one, "To sell me cosmetics." The diversity of the answers fails to open the mother's eyes. It does not even occur to her to doubt her Melibea, but she does admonish the girl not to receive the shady old woman in her absence. The maid-servant remarks compassionately, "Too late does our mistress think of it." But the daughter, with the rebelliousness that the new experience of being in love has instilled in her, retorts sarcastically feigning submission: "Is she one of those? Nevermore! I am very happy, my lady, that you tell me about her, so I shall know against whom I should be on my guard." Celestina hastens to find Calisto. The day before, Pármeno had succeeded in putting off the gift of a cloak and skirt. As a consequence, when she announces the new victory, Calisto hands over to her a much richer reward, the gold chain which he wears around his neck. This reward inflames the greed of the servants as the cloak and skirt could never have done.

At the rendezvous Melibea puts Calisto to the test: she pretends to have summoned him only to dissuade him from his love. Calisto's grief, in his almost innocent selfishness, is so intense that Melibea takes maternal pity on him, confesses her love, and arranges a meeting in her garden for the following night. Her father has heard the steps and voices, and questions her. She eludes her predicament by another quick lie, but the words which she uses to describe to her maid her parents' reaction no longer contain that sarcasm with which she responded to her mother the day before, but rather something like a glimmer of remorse. In the meantime, the servants rush to Celestina's house to demand their share of her takings. The old woman, so skillful in manipulating other people's passions, lets herself be blinded by her own — her greed; she fails to discern the seriousness of the situation, and persists in contradictory lies, in futile promises. She repeats the manœuvres with which she has scored successes on other occasions, bringing up again, for example, the infamy of Pármeno's mother. But precisely this innuendo causes the youth's accumulated rancor to erupt. He spurs his accomplice, and despite Elicia's screams, they murder Celestina and try to flee, jumping from the window just as the law-officers arrive and catch them.

In the following act, as Calisto lazily awakens, he remembers the conversation with Melibea. Because of his defective sense of reality

— an essential pecularity of his — he calls the servants who accompanied him, to make certain that the conversation really occurred. The servants, of course, are unavailable. In their place arrives the young page, Tristán; and a little later the groom, Sosia, spreads the terrible news: Sempronio and Pármeno have been executed. For a moment, Calisto shudders at the thought of the scandal and the disgrace, but, dominated by his hopes for the new rendezvous, he callously substitutes this team of servants for the dead ones. At night he scales the high walls of Melibea's garden, obtains her love and — as reported in the definitive version — returns, silently and wearily, to immure himself in the "solitude and silence and darkness" of his bedroom or, rather, of his conscience. After a painful and laborious meditation he manages again to draw away from reality, to dismiss his scruples, and revive his love.

While he delves, dissatisfied, into his soul, his servants, believing him asleep, admire from the window a "pretty lass," who enters to visit another: they are Elicia and Areúsa. The one is quarrelling with the braggart Centurio, whom she keeps. The visitor brings the news of their friends' and mother Celestina's death. The grief of both prostitutes heightens their grudge against Melibea, first manifested in the feast scene of Act IX. They decide to punish Calisto so "Melibea may cry as much as she is now enjoying herself." The instrument of their vengeance is Centurio whom his mistress, against her better judgment, deems both valiant and infatuated with her. The other tool is the simpleton Sosia from whom, on pretext of recommending discretion, she learns the exact time and place of the next assignation. An amused Centurio laughs at the two sluts, assuming the role of champion-knight at the orders of the lady of his thoughts. But after humbugging them with his bravado, he thinks above all of how to shed his promise. He succeeds in this by entrusting a chum of his to make a big noise to frighten Calisto's servants. Meanwhile, Melibea's parents, unaware of what is happening, contemplate marrying her off, and extol her virtue and filial obedience. Lucrecia, sympathetic and mocking, listens to their illusions. At the sight of Lucrecia, Melibea also lends an ear, unshaken and defiant in her love. The two old people deliberate: would it be suitable, asks the father, who has none of Capulet's despotism, "to allow her to choose a husband as the laws permit?" The mother answers (XVI, 162 f.):

"What are you saying? Why are you wasting your time? Who would break such news to our Melibea without frightening her? Why! Do you think she knows what men are, if they marry or what marriage means?

. . . Don't believe it, Sir Pleberio. . . . Well I know the daughter I have reared so carefully."

Melibea, tortured, orders Lucrecia to interrupt the conversation of her parents under any pretext.

The lovers meet again, with tender confidence, with a much more harmonious and intimate love, with a peacefulness which permits them to sense the beauty and enchantment of the surrounding night. Their caresses and remonstrances, enviously commented upon by Lucrecia, are interrupted by the shouts of the servants, who react with courage to the noise of the ruffians dispatched by Centurio. But Calisto knows that only the inexperienced groom and the young page are there to guard him. So, following for once the call of duty and generosity, he hurries to their rescue, trips and falls from the ladder. Melibea's distress is so desperate that she casts aside all caution. It is Lucrecia who leads her to her room, and tells her master that his daughter is suddenly ill. With deep concern, Pleberio proposes medicines and amusements; his words suggest to Melibea a plan for her death. Pretending to agree, she goes up to the tower, from which she keeps Pleberio and Lucrecia away on various pretexts. Alone at the top of the tower, she confesses to her father all that has happened, with the frankness of one who has nothing to lose; and once her confession is finished, she hurls herself over the edge. At the sight of the corpse, her mother swoons, and her father utters a long lamentation which includes no moralizing but does convey the sombre message of the *Tragicomedy.*

Thus, the events marking the configuration of the simple plot are vindicated by minute factual circumstances traceable to the environment, by inevitable consequences of the characters' doings, by results of essential personality traits, by emotional impulses. Each word, each action ties in, logically and psychologically, with the others, achieving — with astonishingly few exceptions[12] — a realistic coherence, uni-

---

[12] These exceptions include: the protagonists' chance meeting in Act I, the intervention of Celestina, and the use of magic. The most important is the second or, to put it differently, the fact that Calisto and Melibea behave as though they were precluded from the prospect of legitimately fulfilling their love. The reason for this situation is, I believe, that the only literary pattern then existing for a tragic love depicted with artistic sympathy, was the illicit relation we find in troubadouresque lyric, *roman courtois,* and romances of chivalry. For contemporary readers of *The Celestina,* who shared its authors' literary background, and were familiar with the rôle of the go-between in actual life, the lapse was less obvious: in fact, the objection was not raised by early critics of the play. Besides, Calisto's character — though not Melibea's — palliates this shortcoming, to a certain extent. For a detailed discussion of this question, see *La originalidad artística de "La Celestina,"* Ch. VIII.

versally valid, and independent of the drama's literary and historical background. Now we understand why the authors of *The Celestina* rejected the intricate plot of Roman comedy and its modern reverberations, and needed twenty-one acts to set before the reader their extremely simple story. True, the authors are silent about their reasons for selecting the ample scale of humanistic comedy. But no less a literary figure than Benito Pérez Galdós proclaimed these reasons in so many words when returning to the dramatic form of *The Celestina*.[13] "Let us grant space to the truth," pleaded Galdós in the Prologue to his drama *Soul and Life,* 1902, "to the psychology, above all to the construction of characters, to the details needed for describing life." That is: what prompted Pérez Galdós to adopt the unusual form of *The Celestina* was the desire for true-to-life presentation requiring the "space" which in his own century the novel, but not the drama, possessed; and which in the fifteenth century the humanistic comedy rather than the novel boasted — that "space" which *The Celestina* expands in a truly "marvelous way."

[13] Very likely, the eclipse of humanistic comedy has been the main reason for classifying *The Celestina* as a dialogue or, more often, as a dramatic novel. So far as I know, before 1700 no critic raised any doubt about its dramatic form; also, it exerted special influence on dramatic works, some of them actually put on the stage. But from the early eighteenth century, critics steeped in neoclassical codification of art forms objected to the play's unusual length and to its free handling of space and movement. This is why the unknown authors of the English adaptation printed in Vol. II of *The Life of Guzman d'Alfarache,* London, 1707, choosing as their motto Horace's precept "neue minor quinto, neu sit productior actu / fabula," branded *The Celestina* as "a Monster to the Conduct, unworthy the Name of a Tragedy, Comedy, Tragicomedy, . . . it having no less than 21 Acts," and ultimately declared the work to be "properly Dramatical Dialogues." By 1738, an obscure French compiler, Louis-Adrien Du Perron de Castera, asserted in his collection of Spanish plays that works like *The Celestina* were at their very best "des Romans en Dialogues," a formula which reflects the well-known tendency of neoclassical criticism to label as novel anything refractory to the Aristotelian and Horatian tripartite classification of epic, lyric, and drama. Spanish neoclassical critics, in turn, adopted the formula, and their greatest spokesman, Leandro Fernández de Moratín (1760-1828), gave it (not without misgivings) a widespread currency, at home and abroad: "la novela dramática intitulada *Celestina*" (*Orígenes del teatro español,* Madrid, 1830 [posthumous edition], p. 26). For most readers of our own time, the novelistic features of *The Celestina* are its length and its individualistic, detailed presentation of physical and psychological reality — that is, the very features for which *The Celestina* is specifically indebted to humanistic comedy. These traits likewise happen to characterize modern novels, as created by Stendhal, Dickens, Tolstoy, but, in sober fact, are conspicuously absent from the chivalresque and sentimental novel familiar to the authors of the *Tragicomedy.* For a detailed study of *The Celestina*'s literary genre and its bearing on Pérez Galdós' dramatic theory and practice, see *La originalidad artística de "La Celestina,"* Ch. I.

CHAPTER FIVE

The Celestina: Some Aspects of Its Dramatic Technique

The Celestina was not written to be performed in a theater for the simple reason that there were no theaters in Europe at that time. It was written for recitation, as can be inferred from the Prologue and from a stanza which urges that it be read expressively, modulating the voice to set off the differences of emotion and of character. This negative fact of not aiming at a production on the stage, plus the authors' knowledge of ancient drama (read without archeological trammels), plus their familiarity with medieval drama, account for the liberty of the imaginary staging; a liberty which leads to an astounding verisimilitude. The authors have supplied the indications necessary for visualizing the scene and the changes of scene, the personages, their movements and gestures; they have supplied the monologues, and especially the asides, with a distinctly more realistic touch. They have diversified the dialogues, from the oratorical type (which in its winding sentences adequately encompasses the *double entendre,* the insinuation, and the doubt) to the very laconic dialogue in which the accomplices reach an understanding.[1] And precisely

---

[1] Monologues are not, as is often the case in Latin comedy, expositions of the story, programs of action, descriptions of scenes not actually performed, or biographical sketches of the characters, all with a view to clarifying the intricacies of the plot for the benefit of the audience. They are rather outlets for emotional outbursts (II, 125 f.; V, 193 ff.), instances of psychological delving into the speaker's mind (XIV, 132 ff.) or of conflict between clashing loyalties (I, 37 ff.; X, 53 ff.). Asides are most often perceived by those characters they are not meant for, and the degree of perception varies according to the interlocutors' mood: Calisto, for instance, fails to notice the conversation carried in asides by his servants as long as he and Celestina are speaking about Melibea, but he does grow aware of it the moment Celestina mentions her torn cloak and her hopes for a better one (VI, 210 f.). Besides the oratorical (II, 113 ff., IV, 175 ff., etc.) and the *staccato* dialogues (I, 60; I, 111; X, 66, etc.), one may set off the dialogue where one speaker's incisive repartee elicits a prolix reply from the other (I, 46 ff.; VII, 247 ff., etc.), and the dialogue of moderate length, achieving a "natural" and "modern" effect; this last type, which quantitatively predominates throughout the *Tragicomedy,* marks perhaps its most important contribution to sixteenth-century Spanish drama in prose. For a fuller analysis of these and the other aspects of *The*

because it was not destined for the stage, *The Celestina* jealously maintains the theatrical illusion. It rejects, for example, the artificial types of dialogue — the lyrical counterpoint so dear to Calderón or the epigrammatic counterpoint which pleased Molière. The authors do not interrupt the performance to face the public — as happens frequently in Plautus — and carefully avoid pointing out that the show is a play and not real life — a device resorted to by Terence, Shakespeare, Lope de Vega, Calderón and many others. The authors of *The Celestina*, and Fernando de Rojas in particular, concentrate all their efforts on creating the theatrical illusion,[2] a goal which is the

Celestina's dramatic technique, see the corresponding chapters in *La originalidad artística de "La Celestina."*

[2] This is why *The Celestina* avoids the debate — a favorite with ancient and medieval playwrights: some situations, for which the debate was *de rigueur,* are rendered in the *Tragicomedy* in highly dramatic scenes, functionally connected with the remainder of the play. Compare the debate between the heroine and the old woman in Roman tragedy (*Agamemno,* vv. 141 ff.; *Hercules Œtaeus,* 233 ff.; *Medea,* 116 ff.; *Octauia,* 75 ff.), and the dramatic dialogue between Melibea and Celestina (IV, 165 ff.; X, 55 ff.); the farcical debate between servants in Roman comedy (*Asinaria,* vv. 297 ff., 545 ff.; *Mostellaria,* 1 ff.; *Persa,* 272 ff.; *Pseudolus,* 358 ff., 912 ff.; *Rudens,* 938 ff.), and the conversations between Sempronio and Pármeno (VIII, 9 ff.; IX, 25 ff.; XII, 84 ff.), Sosia and Tristán (XIII, 115 f.; XIV, 127 f., 139 f.; XIX, 187 ff.). Farcical dialogues are by no means absent from Modern Age theater: cf. Shakespeare, *The Comedy of Errors,* III, 1; *The Two Gentlemen of Verona,* II, 3; Lope de Vega, *Amar sin saber a quién* [The Unknown Beloved], I, 10; Calderón, *Antes que todo es mi dama* [My Lady Comes First], I, 1, etc. Equally avoided is the unrealistic dialogue presenting interlocutors who comically speak at cross purposes, as in Plautus, *Aulularia,* vv. 731 ff. (a scene imitated in Molière's *L'Avare,* V, 3), where the lover refers to the miser's daughter, while the miser refers to his pot of money. Neither do we find dialogues achieving humoristic effect through repetition of the same utterance by one or more speakers, as in Plautus, *Casina,* vv. 406 ff.; *Poenulus,* 428 ff.; *Pseudolus,* 483 ff.; *Rudens,* 1212 ff.; *Trinummus,* 583 ff.; Terence, *Phormio,* 353 f., 373 f., 437-440; cf. Lope de Vega, *El mejor alcalde, el rey* [The King Is the Best Judge], III, 7 and 8, and some of Molière's most famous scenes, such as *Les Fourberies de Scapin,* II, 7; *Tartuffe,* I, 4; *Le Misanthrope,* I, 2.

Roman dramatists quite often cause a break in the theatrical illusion by addressing directly the audience instead of the other characters, either in long speeches and monologues (see n. 1), or in asides which function as a running commentary not integrated with the corresponding scenes (Plautus, *Asinaria,* vv. 265 ff.; *Casina,* 685 ff.; *Mostellaria,* 157 ff.; Terence, *Eunuchus,* 265): I know of only one case of such an aside in the whole *Celestina,* and it characteristically pertains to Act I, 44. Plautus is rather fond of rupturing the theatrical illusion by pointing up the technical circumstances of the performance; thus, in *Poenulus,* vv. 550 ff., the hired witnesses reply to the character who sets about to coach them: "We know all that already — if only the spectators know . . . , they're the ones for you to instruct . . . Don't bother about us: . . . we all learned our lines along with you, so as to be able to talk back to you" (P. Nixon's translation, *Loeb's Classical Library,* IV, Cambridge, Mass., 1951, p. 55); cf. too *Bacchides,* 212 ff.; *Curculio,* 462 ff.;

cause and effect of their artistic ideal: life-like realism. Let us examine some aspects of this effort.

STAGE DIRECTIONS. *The Celestina* handles the stage directions as artistic subject-matter, incorporating them into the very text of the drama. For practical purposes, the great variety of such directions may be grouped into four principal patterns. The enunciative directions simply declare the presence or the actions of a personage. Thus, Celestina, who has promised Pármeno possession of Areúsa, states as they are approaching the girl's house (VII, 244): "I shall go up." But we seldom find in the *Tragicomedy* the dry enunciative tone so

Mercator, 160; *Persa,* 59 f.; *Pseudolus,* 388. Nor is modern theater adverse to such humorous situations: witness Alessandro Piccolomini's delightful play *L'amor costante,* whose personages overstep incessantly the line between stage and audience and, in Spanish Golden Age *comedia,* the *gracioso's* frequent direct address to the public.

The purposeful breaking of the theatrical illusion by means of literary innuendo is frequent both in Plautus and in Terence; thus, in the former's *Bacchides,* vv. 694 ff., the slave, while devising a trick, disparages slaves' tricks in comedies (cf. *Amphitruo,* 987 ff.; *Casina,* 64, 860 f., 1006; *Captiui,* 778 f.; Terence, *Hecyra,* 866 ff., etc.); for medieval literature directly bearing on *The Celestina,* suffice it to remember the *Book of Good Love,* stanza 698, where Sir Melon praises Convent-trotter's help by placing it above Venus' help to Pamphilus, i.e., by hinting at the actual source of Sir Melon's story. Such devices have been popular in the extreme with Modern Age dramatists (Ariosto, *I suppositi,* II, 2; V, 8; *La lena,* III, 1; Shakespeare, *Love's Labours Lost,* V, last scene; *Twelfth Night,* III, 4; Lope de Vega, *Santiago el Verde* [Green Saint James], II, 3; *La fuerza lastimosa* [The Piteous Compulsion], III, 19, etc.) and very specially with Calderón: take, from among numerous instances available, *No hay burlas con el amor* [Do not Toy with Love], II, 13, and *La desdicha de la voz* [The Luckless Voice], II, 16, where one of the characters underlines the similarity of certain situations with scenes "in the comedies by Don Pedro Calderón." Calderón is, in fact, the very antithesis of the authors of *The Celestina:* while these set to write a play suggestive of reality, Calderón envisaged reality as a play — a vision present in many of his works and culminating in his religious masterpiece *El gran teatro del mundo* [All the World's a Stage]. For more recent examples, see Gogol, *The Inspector,* V, 8; Ibsen, *Peer Gynt,* V, 2. In Pirandello's *Sei personaggi in cerca d'autore* and Wilder's *The Skin of Our Teeth,* the sophisticated structure of the play within the play is essential — as it was for Beaumont and Fletcher, *The Knight of the Burning Pestle.* Not only is there nothing of the sort in *The Celestina,* but we are able to gauge its authors' serious endeavor to avoid any suggestion of the theatrical nature of their work, which might detract from its illusionistic realism. In *Pseudolus,* vv. 1081 ff., a *leno* decries the injuries he has received: "Stage patter, the regular line of abuse a pimp gets in the comedies, stuff boys know: told me I was vile and villainous and perjured" (P. Nixon's translation, *ibidem,* p. 257); compare the obvious imitation of the passage in *Celestina,* VI, 213, where, however, the two allusions to the theatre have been carefully suppressed. For a fully documented study of *The Celestina*'s avoidance of the rupture of dramatic illusion, see my forthcoming paper, "Algunos elementos de la comedia y la novela antigua y medieval ausentes en *La Celestina.*"

frequent in Roman comedy and in its medieval offshoots. Read in its context, this type of stage direction is almost invariably so colored as to suggest at once the intention, desire, fear and hope of the character who utters it. In the case cited, Celestina's full statement reads:

I shall go up and see what can be done in the matter at hand, and with good luck we shall do more than either you or I are planning.

The kind of enunciative stage-direction that predominates in the *Tragicomedy* is one disguised as command, request, query or greeting. Celestina puts an end to the second conference with Melibea by saying (X, 66): "Goodbye, for your mother is coming." Here "goodbye" implies "I'm leaving," and the rest not only indicates Alisa's arrival but indicates that her presence, which both Celestina and Melibea dread, is the cause of the old woman's departure. It would be otiose to stress the importance that this enunciative stage direction has in the treatment of place. It underlines the continuity of the action as well as its shift in space, now *en route,* now through different settings, passing from one or more indoor scenes to the street, and back again — an unthinkable state of affairs in the classical theater.

A second type, the descriptive stage-direction, quite varied and abundant, reflects the authors' lively attention to the appearance and gestures of the characters, to the material circumstances which frame the action and instill concreteness into the dialogue. As a result we envisage, for instance, Celestina, an old hag, painted (I, 66), bearded (III, 127), toothless (IX, 41), with a sinister scar crossing her once beautiful face (IV, 170 ff.), dragging her threadbare cloak and ragged skirt (VI, 203 ff.). Or another example: Thanks to Melibea's words of welcome to Calisto in the last rendezvous, we see her garden by moonlight, and we hear the ripple of its fountain and the rustle of the breeze that sways its cypresses (XIX, 194).

A third type of stage-direction, sometimes indicative of the presence or action of a character, then again briefly descriptive, is inferred from the dialogue instead of being explicitly stated. Thus, as she enters Alisa's drawing-room, Celestina greets the lady, who has already spoken up in the previous scene. But she likewise salutes Melibea, whose presence we suddenly conjecture from the salutation (IV, 161). A glance at this type of stage-direction shows that Rojas has systematically used it to evade the direct presentation of risqué scenes. Calisto's amorous impatience, for example, transpires obliquely through Melibea's complaints against his saucy hands (XIV, 126; XIX, 195).

Finally, there exists that kind of stage-direction which is tied up with the action and with the characters. This variety receives a multiform and subtle elaboration, since the perfect interplay of actions and motives and the minute delineation of the characters have presided over the composition of the *Tragicomedy*. A single example: in Act VI, 225, Celestina, after telling Calisto about her interview with Melibea, tries to withdraw, but he detains her, eager to continue the conversation about his beloved. Pármeno, hostile to both and not at all sentimental, imposes his will in an aside to Sempronio (who listens sentimentally to the report), in order to alert Celestina, so that she should put an end to their master's chatter.

Pármeno: Now, listen, Sempronio. I want to whisper something in your ear.
Sempronio: Well, what is it?
Pármeno: This attentive listening of Celestina's induces our master to protract his talk. Go near her, tap her with your foot. Let us signal her to tarry no longer, but to leave.

The complexity of the scene deserves close attention; a first stage-direction marks the beginning of the aside. A second describes "this attentive listening of Celestina's," one of her crafty pretenses, since, with this show of sympathy, she inspires confidence in Calisto. The third recommends a gesture that is then carried out, for soon after we read Celestina's whispered answer:

I understand, Sempronio. Just let him alone; he'll come to his senses. He is finishing.

In addition, this brief passage points up the eloquent ecstasy of the lovesick youth, the rancorous impatience of one servant, the passivity of the other, and the adaptability of the astute go-between.

A trait very peculiar to the *Tragicomedy* is its perfectly free handling of place and time, both governed only by the logic of the subject-matter, without consideration of any external factor. One finds as many locales as the movement of the characters requires, not only those which the staging can afford. As much time elapses as the events sketched in the dialogue plausibly require for each action, with little regard for the length of the performance or for the precepts of the critics.[3] Let me emphasize the negative circumstances of this solution: on the one hand, *The Celestina* antecedes the montage of the modern theater; on the other, it precedes the polemic revolving around a

[3] For my interpretation of time and place in *The Celestina* I am much indebted to Professor Stephen Gilman, "El tiempo y el género literario en *La Celestina*," *Revista de Filología Hispánica*, VII (1945), 149 ff.; *The Art of "La Celestina*," Madison, Wis., 1956, pp. 105 ff., 114, 137 ff. Professor Manuel J. Asensio, "El tiempo en *La Celestina*," *Hispanic Review*, XX (1952), 28 ff., has also been helpful.

play's unities, a polemic launched by the Italian interpreters of Aristotle's *Poetics*. The upshot of that controversy is that even today it takes us an effort to rid ourselves of the notion that the time and place of the play must match those of the spectator.

PLACE. The aversion of the *Tragicomedy* to any "streamlining" of reality entails its very numerous settings, which one can infer from the dialogue. Thus, in addition to other houses, we become acquainted with Celestina's at the end of the city, remote and half crumbling (I, 69 f.), but noisy with music, songs, knife-fights, and scandals (XVII, 165). We view its swept doorway (XVII, 167), its loft for keeping brooms (and for hiding one customer upon the unexpected arrival of another: I, 60 ff.), its garret on top of the sun-gallery (which contains the equipment for Celestina's witchcraft: III, 142 ff.), its upstairs bedrooms accommodating the old woman and Elicia (III, 147; XII, 101, 109), its dining-room below, contiguous to the street door (IX, 27). We familiarize ourselves with the city, its marketplace, where criminals are executed and bullfights are arranged (XIII, 115). We learn a good deal about the churches and convents (I, 71; IV, 164; VIII, 19; IX, 25, 47; XI, 69; XII, 96), and about the streets, endangered by dogs, holes and causeways (XIV, 124), shaken by the din of the police beat, and illuminated suddenly by people passing with torches (XII, 96, 98). Then we visualize the city's outskirts bordering the river, with their tanneries and their rundown houses of ill repute (I, 69 f.; IV, 160). These settings have no existence previous to the action, as has been the case with the props indicated in realistic drama since the nineteenth century. Rather, they are silhouetted as the course of the action requires, and, in many instances, they cleverly complement it. The windows of Celestina's house, for example, open suddenly, at the precise instant in which, after the assassination, the neighbors and the law-officers rush in (XII, 111). Only in the following act, on describing the lamentable state in which Pármeno and Sempronio were found after jumping through them, are we told that they were "very high windows" (XIII, 119), in order to point up the more effectively the desperation of the murderers. The characters of *The Celestina*, then, act not in an abstract vacuum, like the monochromatic background of primitive medieval painting, but in settings interior and exterior, of close and of distant perspective, which the authors pictured with the concreteness of backgrounds in contemporary Hispano-Flemish painting.[4]

[4] In some respects contemporary Hispano-Flemish painting strikingly mirrors *The Celestina*'s handling of space, especially the use of simultaneous scenes,

Not only does *The Celestina* surpass the Spanish Comedy of the Golden Age and the Elizabethan drama in the sheer number of its settings, but its complex and original use of stage directions creates a dynamic backdrop, so to speak, which helps us actualize the movements of the characters in their natural continuity. Thanks to this technique, *The Celestina* is apt to portray each person in his privacy: Calisto is seen in his room, given over to tears, meditation, or music and poetry; Areúsa, ailing or indulging in sensual pleasure in her perfumed bed; Pleberio and Alisa, brooding over their daughter's welfare. Another consequence is that the *Tragicomedy,* to represent simultaneous situations, prefers to reduce the use of the unrealistic aside, and to alternate the dialogue between different groups of people. Thus in Act XVI, the parents, who deliberate on marrying off Melibea, at first occupy the foreground, then make way for the dialogue between Lucrecia and Melibea, trivial at the outset, later of increased weight, as a result of the heroine's excitement. The words of the young women, in turn, yield to a new dialogue between the parents; and then Melibea and Lucrecia reappear to close the act at highest pitch. Compared with this sophisticated mastery, the cinematic convention which uses close-ups to convey the greater attention bestowed on this or that group of speakers seems primitive indeed.

TIME. Among the many notes of the *Tragicomedy* strangely in tune with our own age, there is one which can never be sufficiently emphasized: its acute awareness of time. Celestina, by way of sly introduction to her message, points out the passage of time, which has destroyed her beauty (IV, 164). While Calisto is recovering his composure he deplores the "wretched sweetness of this most fleeting life" (XIV, 133). The quick pace of time induces, too late, Pleberio and Alisa to marry off Melibea, who defends her privilege to love because she too feels herself harrowed by the pressure of time (XVI, 155 ff.). Such a feeling is another facet of the engrossment of *The Celestina* with life, which reduces death and the beyond to negative concepts without an existence of their own. From the first page to the last, the young people live in quivering expectation. Calisto grows impatient because Sempronio does not rush to bring Celestina to him, and because Pármeno delays opening the door for them; and when Celestina

passage from indoors to outdoors backgrounds, and the like. Presumably it provides the key to the proper interpretation of "the delightful view of the ships" (Act XX, 206) — a favorite background with Flemish and Spanish fifteenth-century painters — and of the clouded sky (Act XIX, 194) unusual in "literary" gardens: cf. C. H. Post, *A History of Spanish Painting,* V, Cambridge, Mass., 1934, pp. 148, 162 f.

returns from her mission, he awaits her in true agony. Then, because she uses circumlocutions to enhance the importance of her success, he begs her (VI, 204): "Mother mine, either be brief or take this sword and kill me." His servants, ready to scoff at his impatience to win Melibea's love, are no less impatient when it comes to their own affairs, and so is Melibea.

Aside from the elegiac musing on the flight of time and the young people's feverish rush, the *Tragicomedy* expresses this concern through a profuse specification of time, comparable only to the specific localizations of the action. It is not an indefinite lapse, but rather the exact span of three days which Sempronio has passed without visiting Celestina and Elicia. It is two years — two decisive years of adolescence — since Melibea last saw Celestina. Calisto's feigned toothache is supposed to have been paining him for eight days, and the patient is precisely twenty-three years old (IV, 186 ff.). The peculiarity of the characters in *The Celestina,* to be each endowed with a history as individuals — a peculiarity unknown to Latin theater and medieval novel — supports these indications of time and projects them into the distant past.

It is likewise surprising to find throughout the *Tragicomedy* a keen awareness of the time of day. Celestina wants to return because it is nightfall (VI, 216). Pármeno awakens alarmed at seeing that it is "broad daylight" (VIII, 8). The servants are alert to the hour of their dinner invitation (IX, 25). In addition, the exact hour is given for many happenings whether or not they are actually displayed. Sempronio has been waiting for Celestina "since one o'clock" (V, 196). Celestina and Melibea agree that the first rendezvous is to be held "when the clock strikes twelve" (X, 66; XI, 74); and from eleven sharp Calisto keeps watch on the strokes of the clock, testing the vigilance of the servants in an interlude which pitilessly ridicules the lover's impatience (XII, 81 ff.). But Calisto's soliloquy, after having obtained Melibea's love (XIV, 138), gives artistic relevancy to the clock in one of the most intense situations of modern theater, very much germane to that of Doctor Faustus in the concluding scenes of Marlowe's tragedy. Calisto, much like Doctor Faustus, faces the clock — ironically, created by man himself — as if confronting the impassive face of Nature, indifferent to his anguish and his desire. Yet, for Marlowe man's situation before the clock is a conflict of moral theology, and he paints his hero as overcome with fear of having to pay for "the vaine pleasure of twenty-four yeares" with the torment whose endlessness is underlined by Faustus' desperate bargaining. The

Tragicomedy defines man's situation before the clock as a cosmological and psychological conflict. What tortures Calisto is the regular march of Nature, ingeniously marked by the hands on the dial, with no allowance made for the arbitrariness of the human soul. And between the steady pace of the external world and the impetus of desire, no other bridge is left for Calisto than to revive the past in his memory and to anticipate the future in what he invokes as "sweet imagination," that is, to beguile the waiting and to annul time.

Modern theater schematizes the passage of time just as it schematizes the unfolding of space. At its freest, it lets time run in the interval between one act and another, as Lope de Vega recommended,[5] and as Shakespeare did, notably, in *Henry V*. There the choruses, inserted in the action, supply the space appealing to the imagination of the public, and report the events occurring between the acts. The monologue of Time (of dubious authorship) in *The Winter's Tale*, IV, 1, corresponds exactly to devices also present in various works by Cervantes, Lope, and Calderón.[6] The representation of time in *The*

[5] In his *Arte nuevo de hacer comedias* [A New Art to Write Comedies], vv. 199 ff., where he gives advice with a mixture of compunction and mockery — his peculiar reaction to the tyranny of Italian preceptists —: "When the poet writes about a story in which some years have to elapse, he may place them in the distances between two acts." He adhered to his own rule in *Las paces de los reyes y judía de Toledo* [The Reconciliation of the Sovereigns and the Jewess from Toledo], for instance; in Act I, King Alfonso VIII is a child, in Act II he marries Eleanor of England, and falls in love with the Jewess Rachel, and in Act III, after seven years of this love, the noblemen murder Rachel.

[6] Act II of Cervantes, *El rufián dichoso* [The Blessed Ruffian] begins with a dialogue in which Comedy explains to Curiosity that she was but "now" (i.e., during Act I) in Seville, enacting the profane life of the protagonist, who then had his conversion in Toledo, and at present lives as a pious friar in Mexico. Then she adds: "I have joined Mexico with Seville in one moment, sewing up this and the third part of the play to the first one." In Act I of Lope de Vega, *El Perseo* [Perseus], Jupiter who has just visited Danae, commands Time to move onward nine months, so that Perseus' birth should prevent his mother's marriage to an unworthy suitor. Act I of Calderón, *Origen, pérdida y restauración de la Virgen del Sagrario* [Origin, Loss and Restoration of the Virgin of the Sagrario] takes place at Saint Ildefonso of Toledo's time (middle of seventh century); at its end, the *gracioso* Payo, in the poet's name, extends to the audience an invitation to attend the next Act, underlining the passage of time and the change in people and custom; Act II takes place during the Arabs' invasion of Spain (early eighth century) and, at its end, the Toledan Godmán conceals the Virgin, predicting her future triumph; in Act III, the Queen of Castile, wife of Alfonso VI, and the Archbishop of Toledo (late eleventh century) find the image and restore it to its cult. Even closer to the monologue in *The Winter's Tale* is the situation in *San Francisco de Borja, Duque de Gandía* [Saint Francis Borgia, Duke of Gandía], a play attributed to Father Pedro de Fomperosa and presumably

Celestina is far removed from such rigidity and such subterfuges. First of all, one detects no strict correspondence between the duration of the different actions. Pármeno, for example, pronounces his long report on Celestina (I, 66 ff.) while the latter and Sempronio, after having knocked at the door, are waiting to be admitted. It is clear that in naturalistic terms the detailed word-picture of Celestina is too long to fit into the interval between her arrival and her entrance, although it does fit "impressionistically," as a kind of temporal close-up.

Comparable to this impressionistic, nonobjective use of time in simultaneous actions is the implicit indication of passage of time even though this passage has not been enacted before the reader. In Act II, 116, for example, Sempronio lets it be understood that the ravings to which Calisto has delivered himself in Act I are no unusual occurrence. Similarly, without an express warning that this is no longer the opening day, Pármeno refers to the falcon, the drama's starting point, as lost "the other day." When Melibea acknowledges defeat, she confesses to Celestina (X, 64) : "Many, many days have passed since that noble gentleman spoke to me of love," though the text has in fact shown only one day and one night. The insistence with which Rojas refers to this implicit time points to the motive of his curious procedure: to make likely, within the bounds of her character, Melibea's surrender to her love, which would have seemed inconceivable if, after angrily rejecting Calisto on the morning of the first day, she should have yielded to him on the afternoon of the next. Juan Ruiz too had suggested scenes, rather than actually narrate them, to soften the change in Lady Sloe's emotions. Melibea's psychological evolution requires the amorous service of "many, many days," which cause her feelings to mature until the moment at which Celestina's skill elicits a decision already made.

One important consequence of this fact dawns upon us: drawn-out as it may be, the action of the *Tragicomedy* supplies no faithful record of everything that happens from the minute Calisto's falcon enters Melibea's garden. No matter how much the eating, sleeping, nightfall or daybreak, which serve to mark off segments of the action, create the illusion that everything unfolds before the eyes of the reader, the action projected in *The Celestina* is not the uninterrupted flow of

based on a lost play by Calderón. There Act III opens with a dialogue between Virtue and Time; the latter is ordered to tell all that happened to the Saint during four years "tying up the thread that was broken" at the end of Act II, an order fulfilled in full detail.

reality, but rather a typical selection from it, which at no point coincides with the continuous sequence of life. No matter how deft and searching may be the portrayal of the souls in their utterances, these speeches are mere milestones set up at fairly long intervals, milestones between which the characters mature and change. This peculiar representation of time in the *Tragicomedy* is essential because it answers two primary needs: the desire to reflect reality by suggesting the proper moment for each action, and the striving after psychological plausibility by allowing sufficient time for the evolution of those characters that develop within the drama.

The conception of reality, no longer as providentially ruled by a code which its Maker's will can suspend, as Juan Ruiz believed, but as an irrevocable continuum of causes and effects, takes shape in *The Celestina* through two other systematic procedures, already mentioned: irony and parallelism.

IRONY. What the personages say or do is meaningful as a direct reaction to the immediate situational context. But for the reader who, unlike the personages, knows the truth in every aspect and at each turn of the drama, what is said or done carries an additional meaning, tied to the basic outline of the work and, in particular, to its tragic ending. We may recall, as an example of verbal irony, the verse in which Othello guarantees with his life Desdemona's fidelity and affirms Iago's integrity:

> My life upon her faith! Honest Iago,

without suspecting that the latter's perfidy will lead him to believe Desdemona unfaithful and, in consequence, will cause the loss of his life. Amid the profusion of cases which the *Tragicomedy* offers, let us mention the words with which Celestina wishes to dispel the suspicion awakened in her accomplice through her imprudent use of the diminutive "small share" (V, 197):

Hush, silly, a small share or a big share, I shall give you as much as you wish. Everything I have is yours. Let us enjoy ourselves, let us make our profit: we shall never quarrel about dividing our gain.

She herself exemplifies the wisdom of her advice, since it is her obstinacy in refusing to share her gain that leads to her own death and to the downfall of her accomplices. Nevertheless, as her words are pronounced deceitfully, the effect is less moving than in the cases exempt from any double meaning; as when Alisa, on leaving her daughter in the company of the disreputable old woman, urges her (IV, 164):

Well, Melibea, gratify our neighbor in everything // it is fair
to pay for her thread.

The pause between the principal and the secondary sentence creates
an equivocation whose tragic intensity recalls verse 928 of *Œdipus the
King,* in which the word-order and the cesura inject an ominous meaning into the innocent phrase with which the Chorus introduces
Jocasta:

This is his wife and mother // of his children.

On hearing that Melibea agrees to a rendezvous, Calisto breaks into a
jubilation that earns him Celestina's prudent remonstrances (XI, 74):

I have always heard that it is more difficult to bear good
fortune than bad.

This is one of the many Petrarchan saws in the play which, far from
being merely stylistic or moralizing, thanks to their irony, in many instances, possess a basic dramatic function. For these words, pronounced
shortly before the old woman receives the fatal gold chain, have their
ironic application to herself. She, who has manipulated the lovers,
servants, and girls with such skill, on taking possession of the unexpected reward, is unable to govern her prosperous fortune, and
through greed, she works her own death.[7] In the concluding assignation, Rojas has piled up ironies which act as premonitions of imminent
disaster. Melibea, whom Calisto catches by surprise as she sings while
waiting for him, mentions modestly that her voice is "hoarse as a
swan's" (XIX, 194). Any reader, led above all by the *Tragicomedy*'s
fondness for the traditional bestiary (Prologue, pp. 19 ff.; IV, 176 ff.),
would grasp the allusion to the beautiful fable of the swan who sings
on sensing that death is near by. Calisto, the impatient dreamer,
always longs for the passage of time. Only a brief instant before dying,
experiencing perfect joy in Melibea's arms, he expresses the desire to
make time come to a stop (XIX, 197): "I wish, Madam, that dawn
would never come. . . . ": and, in fact, it never comes for *him.*

As for the irony of actions or situations, we may recall *Much Ado
About Nothing,* III, 5, where the grotesque constable and head-
borough come to acquaint Leonato with the villain's machination
against his daughter's honor: but in his haste to celebrate the en-
gagement of the latter, Leonato refuses to listen to them, thus exposing
himself to the affront that he might otherwise have avoided. Irony
in the actions is, one might say, the key to Sempronio's moves in the
Tragicomedy: after having named Elicia as the principal reason for
keeping alive, he vehemently warns Calisto against confiding in

[7] Gilman, *The Art of "La Celestina,"* pp. 122 f., 171 ff.

women (I, 37 ff.). In the next scene we witness him declare his passion with no lesser vehemence, which culminates at the very moment when the steps of his hidden rival are heard. In addition, Celestina feeds him with lies, and Elicia toys at deceiving him with half-truths (I, 61 ff.; cf. also III, 142 and IX, 40). There is a stark irony in that it should be the irresolute Sempronio who triggers the drama into movement by introducing Celestina, and that his only action, after this, should consist in assassinating her. Peculiar to the *Tragicomedy* is the ironic contrast between human planning and the fatalistic concatenation of events, which mocks man's futile efforts. Celestina strives to seal the friendship between the two servants, not because of any exalted love of peace, but in order to clear the terrain of adversaries who might keep her from draining Calisto's wealth. What she fails to foresee is that the accomplices, allied through her mediation, will turn against her: it is her own work, the union of Sempronio's seasoned force and Pármeno's youthful malice, that will rob her of her life. Other situations present whole series of ironies. Pármeno spitefully prevents Celestina from receiving the cloak and skirt which Calisto has granted her (VI, 218); as a result, on the following day, Calisto hands over to her the gold chain, the partition of which will cause the death of all (XI, 71 ff.). Pleberio's kindness and solicitude place within reach the possibility of a happy ending, since in marrying off his daughter he plans to let her choose her husband. It is Melibea herself, in her passionate fury, and her mother, utterly ignorant of the daughter whom she fancies she knows so well, who ruin the one possibility, the imminence of which adds to the poignancy of the final catastrophe.

The concluding interpolated acts seem to enjoy ironic contrasts between what man proposes and what God disposes. Not by any chance the disloyal servants, but the loyal Sosia, enticed by the courtesan, provokes the death of the master for whom he willingly risks his life. Calisto, in turn, who believed the cowards Sempronio and Pármeno to be brave, assesses Sosia and Tristán as being weaklings, and kills himself in his needless rush to help them (XIX, 197 ff.). The lovers perish, falling prey to the vengeance of the prostitutes barely familiar to Calisto (I, 43) and totally unknown to Melibea, but who detest Melibea much more than they do Calisto. An essential ingredient in the ludicrousness of Centurio, the instrument of this vengeance, is the ironic discrepancy between his peaceable nature and his chosen job as a professional bully. Intimidated by his fantastic bravado, one of the girls pleads that Calisto be punished, but not killed.

Centurio is a braggart, who only thinks of dodging the agreement at no risk to himself, and this is the strongest guarantee of his harmlessness. Despite everything, death, which no one wishes for Calisto, catches that egoist on the one occasion when he ceases being egoistic. In the elemental war which is our cosmos — *The Celestina* seems to tell us — a human purpose is an accident too small to affect the total interplay of events, and to obtain the solution suiting the individual.

PARALLELISM. As one examines the *Tragicomedy,* the parallelism of characters, sayings, and situations becomes immediately apparent, parallelism of situations being visible also in the conception of the plot and in the technique of its exposition. The author of Act I has Calisto flanked at each side by the two servants, contrasted somewhat sketchily in their character and in their relation with their master and with Celestina. Rojas maintains their individuality but allows Pármeno to evolve, thus lessening the contrast and uniting both servants in the action. This treatment is typical, for the repeated situations, sayings, and characters are never absolutely identical replicas nor are they absolutely opposed to the archetype of their kind. After their death, Sempronio and Pármeno are replaced by Sosia and Tristán, each of whom resembles his predecessor in intellect (with the difference that Sempronio is the erudite and Sosia the ignorant fool), but clashes with him in his morality. Moreover, the new servants differ among themselves. Sosia, naïve and with an amorous disposition, as a matter of principle mistrusts all women, even the noble Melibea; actually, he confides in the most despicable tart, much as did Sempronio. Tristán, though almost a child, is like Pármeno, disillusioned and cautious; but he differs from Pármeno in suffering no resentment or temptation. Elicia and Areúsa are relatives, friends and colleagues, but one resides in Celestina's house, the other is independent. One is peevish, determined, and cunning; the other is imaginative, undecided, and affectionate. Over against them is Lucrecia, of their own class and family, but with a different occupation, honest, faithful to her masters, and not at all passionate. In the acts added in 1502, Centurio compensates, in a way, for the disappearance of Celestina. Like her, he belongs to the underworld, he plies an infamous trade, is devout and eloquent, and dominates his associates by his intelligence. Unlike Celestina, Centurio makes light of his *métier* and his social honor. His devoutness consists not in prayers, but in flamboyant oaths; his eloquence is neither erudite nor moralizing, but has one distinctive touch: its parodic chivalresque tone. He suffers from no greed for wine or money; his passion is gambling, and the only things that he is unable to accomplish are to work or to save money. In comparable situations — that is, in the monologue in which each discourses on the work undertaken — the one stakes her life upon her professional honor, the other shields himself with lies in order to shirk risking his life. The grotesque and tragic Celestina lingers on in the grotesque and comical Centurio, consistently accentuating unity through variation.

The *Tragicomedy* opens with an old-style theological praise of Melibea, which sees in the beauty of the beloved woman the proof of God's greatness. Rojas offers two variations on this solemn beginning, the two differing between themselves, and deviating from the original in tone. One of them is almost a caricature, coming as it does by way of the procuress who, feeling Melibea is weakening, describes Calisto with the words especially used to extol feminine beauty (IV, 188). The other has a somewhat lighter effect, although its humorous cast is unmistakable, since it pertains to the scene which exhibits Calisto's ecstasy in a comical light (VI, 227). Another example: "Oh angelic vision, oh my precious pearl!" exclaims Celestina, to prolong the interview when Melibea is putting an end to it (IV, 172). When embarking on the parallel venture of seducing Areúsa, she calls her "golden pearl," using the more popular variation (VII, 247). "Oh my golden pearls!" is the salutation which she directs at the two servants, who value her wheedling for what it is worth (IX, 27). Calisto's first words on descending the ladder into the arms of Melibea are precisely: "Oh angelic vision, oh my precious pearl, before whom everything else is ugly!" (XIV, 125). The literary flavor of these apostrophes is here stressed: it closely matches Calisto's personality. However, their previous use by Celestina has contaminated the tryst of the two lovers with the recollection of the impure means through which it is being achieved.

Such symmetry in the characters and in their utterances, first suggested then denied, is even more frequent in the situations. Twice, Celestina exhausts her gifts of persuasion in an effort to attract Pármeno to her; the first time in a form all too rationalistic; the second in a form dramatic and emotional. On both occasions she takes refuge in the infamy of the lad's mother, jocularly the first time, vengefully the second. Finally, when bickering with her accomplices, she resorts to the same device, an error that is to cost her this time her life (XII, 109). Twice while *en route* Celestina and Sempronio chat about the love affair hinging on her intercession. The first time Sempronio shows himself apprehensive and timid, while Celestina, though boasting of her aplomb and experience, listens politely to his anxieties. The second time, Celestina, blind with professional pride, hides neither her greed nor the scorn in which she wrongly holds Sempronio. Twice Celestina delivers long monologues. The first time, on her walk toward Melibea's house, she is so fearful that only her sense of professional honor prevails upon her in the chosen course of action; the second time, when returning triumphant after the feared interview. Twice Celestina exercises her artistry as a procuress, identical in purpose, but diverse in the way of adapting herself to two such dissimilar women as Melibea and Areúsa. And twice she practices her lewd medicine, aiding the slut in her hysterical passion and the noble maiden in her faints and heartache, and prescribing the transparently allegorical "herb" suitable for each illness. In their precipitate flight, Sempronio and Pármeno jump from the window of Celestina's house, almost killing themselves in the fall (XII, 111). Calisto dies instantly in the same fashion, when he trips on the ladder (XIX, 198). Melibea, not through necessity or chance, but by free choice, throws herself from her tower (XX, 213). Each of these falls functions as an ill-boding omen of the one which follows, and none is exactly the same as the other two.

Within the simple frame of the plot and the rich detail of its development, the drama advances so dynamically that through their external similarity the parallel situations underline the distance covered. Such is the case of Celestina's two visits to Melibea or of the young couple's two nights of love. Some brief incidental occurrences are no less eloquent. Alisa, for example, on returning home and meeting Celestina (X, 68), finds the same situation which she left the day before, when she departed for her daily visit to her sister, leaving Celestina in Melibea's company (IV, 163 f.). For the reader, however, the deceptive similarity points up the progress in Melibea's emotional commitment that has taken place between the two situations.

Two particular facets of this parallelism relate to the conception and exposition of the plot, and are closely akin to the use of implicit time for suggesting a complete sequence of events not actually performed. To every reader of the *Tragicomedy* the multiplication of obstacles which hinder the conclusion of certain actions seems surprising. Thus, in order to glean all the profit that the seduction of Melibea bids fair to yield, Celestina first has to win over Pármeno, who threatens to alienate her from Calisto; and in order to captivate Pármeno, she must first seize hold of Areúsa, the only means of tempting the adolescent. On the other hand, as we have seen, the seductions of Galatea in *Pamphilus* and of Lady Sloe in the *Book of Good Love* include no such intermediary stages. In *Pamphilus,* the old woman, on casting her net, says, v. 353: "Look, I see Galatea standing at the door." These words are echoed almost literally by those which Celestina pronounces when nearing Melibea's house (IV, 158): "I see Lucrecia at the door." Yet, instead of directly encountering the person whom she was seeking, and of coming right to the point, Celestina must first slip into the confidence of the maid; conducted by her, she arrives before the lady, whose prejudices her wit will likewise have to overcome before she can finally stay in Melibea's presence. In a similar way, the harlots, intent on revenge, delegate the task to the cowardly ruffian, who then delegates it to his chums.

In contrast to Roman comedy and to its modern derivatives, allowing (in deference to the complex intrigue and to the limitations of staging) the actual performance to be often replaced by narration, *The Celestina* hardly contains a single incident which fails to be carried straight to the imaginary stage. Nevertheless, what has already been enacted, is later narrated with new touches which appear to be not fictions added by the narrator, but true details excluded from the previous presentation. In Act III, for example, Celestina tells Sempronio the substance of her dealings with Pármeno in Act I, underscoring her strategy. Again, in Act VI, she reports to Calisto her interview with Melibea, already projected in Act IV, but rounded out with new touches. In Act VIII Pármeno informs Sempronio of his adventure with Areúsa in Act VII, mentioning fine qualities which the girl had no time to show in the actual Act VII. These and many analogous examples seem to disclose Rojas' firm belief that no artistic representation, however circumstantial, can fully reflect the compactness of reality.

Thus, strict motivation, set off by the ironic play of meanings, a fluid concept of time and place, and sustained parallelism, all converge to suggest the infinite variety of life, and the irreducible singularity of each event. For life is not, as Shakespeare would have it, "tedious as a twice-told tale." Rather — if I may quote Heraclitus, cited in the Prologue not without pertinence — it is a perpetual flux and change; nothing in it is a mere mechanical duplication, but a new creation or, in the words of our century's Heraclitus, it is "an original moment in a no less original history."[8]

[8] Henri Bergson, *L'Évolution créatrice,* Paris, 1908, p. 7: "il [each state of mind] est simple, et il ne peut pas avoir été déjà perçu, puisqu'il concentre dans son indivisibilité tout le perçu avec, en plus, ce que le présent y ajoute. C'est un moment original d'une non moins originale histoire."

CHAPTER SIX

The Celestina: The Characters

Among all the dramatic works written in Spanish, the *Tragicomedy of Calisto and Melibea* is unsurpassed in the creation of characters. One of these has cut loose to achieve some sort of autonomy and become one of the mythical figures of Hispanic culture: in popular speech, any astute go-between is called nowadays a "Celestina." But this process is not comparable to the case of Don Juan, who similarly sprang up from Tirso de Molina's *The Seville Deceiver.* There the famous personage is, in truth, the only one deemed worthy of the author's attention. As for the *Tragicomedy,* if the impact of the other characters and, above all, that of the lovers failed to equal Celestina's, this is so because they clash with the accepted conventions and because their rich individuality is not easily reduced to sketchy outlines.

INDIVIDUALITY. Compared with the fixed characters of Roman and elegiac comedy, with the predetermined figures of the religious medieval theater and with the strongly typified personages in the theaters of modern Italy, Spain, and France, the salient trait of the characters of *The Celestina* is their individuality. They are unique creatures, not types, and to enhance this artistic aim, the *Tragicomedy* spares no references to the archetype which serves both as a model and as a foil to the individual variation. Thus, Rojas has been careful to project Celestina against her fellow workers (V, 194), Calisto against love-sick youths (III, 128; IX, 30), Melibea against maidens in love for the first time (III, 137), Lucrecia, faithful and discreet, against thievish and gossipy servants (I, 70; IX, 42). The last example illustrates Rojas' taste for contrasting the individual with his archetype, a taste that has baffled several interpreters when they often found the noble Calisto in unheroic attitudes (I, 40 ff., 91; II, 113; VI, 209, 221, 225 ff.; VIII, 17 ff.; XII, 82 ff.; XIII, 113f., 121); likewise, the high-born Melibea lies to her parents more than once (X, 68; XII, 98; XVI, 163); and conversely, the servants love their paramours with chivalrous exaltation (I, 61; VIII, 15; IX, 39); the prostitute shows traces of modesty (VII, 254 ff.). This is the art of individual variation, for which the work of Juan Ruiz served as a prelude. Thus Juan Ruiz satirized nuns in general, but created the individually blameless Lady Garoza.

Neither is there any attempt to typify the characters according to their social standing — a lack of prejudice which, compared with the almost unanimous practice of medieval and modern literature, shows a hardly less than prodigious originality. For Kaspar von Barth, for example, the German gentleman-scholar who in 1624 translated the *Tragicomedy* into Latin, the ultimate reason for Pármeno's baseness is the vileness inherited from his mother, the notorious Claudina, and inherent in his social station as a servant.[1] Take, however, the servant Sosia, of rustic parentage, who displays a moral and social sense far superior to his master's (XIII, 117 f.; XIV, 128 ff.; XIX, 197 ff.). There are further the discerning Tristán and the judicious Lucrecia to prove that one must not impute to Rojas the prejudices of his translator. A critic as keen as Don Juan Valera could afford to write in this democratic century of ours that the author veiled the pleasures of the aristocratic lovers, while keeping the erotic details for the plebeian ones.[2] This might have been the correct pattern for Valera's biased mind, but hardly so for Rojas, who certainly dealt out the erotic details more profusely in the scenes between the aristocrats than in the scene between the servant and his girl.

Precisely because they are individuals, these creatures are not drawn all at once as in the comedy of types. You will recall how in Molière's *Tartuffe* Act I offers an admirably itemized picture of the hypocrite, and how all his doings and sayings, until the dénouement, only corroborate this already known portrayal. In *The Celestina* the characters emerge slowly from their few deeds and from their many words — confronting others in dialogue and facing themselves in soliloquy — , from the interplay of judgments, and descriptions, often contradictory or misleading, since in them the characters portray not only the person in question but chiefly themselves. Let us examine Melibea's case: at the beginning, Calisto depicts her physical beauty, extolling it according to the canons of traditional rhetoric (I, 54 ff.). At a later stage he ponders on her natural perfection (VI, 226); and right after the first embrace he records her coyness and audacity, as a

---

[1] Apropos of Pármeno's resistance to Celestina's attempts at corrupting him and of his loyalty to Calisto, Barth contends that the actual motivation is his hatred for Sempronio, and elaborates (*Pornoboscodidascalus,* Frankfurt a. M., 1624, p. 349): "Sic neque hic malitiae maternae et seruilis uspiam obliuiscitur" [Thus, he too nowhere forgets the wickedness pertaining to his mother and to his condition as a servant].

[2] "Nueva edición de *La Celestina*" in *El superhombre y otras novedades* [Superman and Other Novelties], Madrid, 1903, pp. 233 f.

maid in her first experience of love (XIV, 139). But others contribute also to the portrait, each with his own touch. Celestina declares that she has known Melibea's home and her mother for a long time; and insinuates that until a short while before, Melibea was an ungainly chit (VI, 225). The rancorous servant Pármeno hints impudently at her attractiveness (II, 124), and the sentimental Sempronio mocks his master but praises his "gracious and lovely Melibea" (IX, 32). These words provoke the fury of the two hussies, who spitefully revile the noble maiden, to the point of reducing her loveliness to costly attire and malodorous salves (IX, 32 ff.). For the new servants Melibea is a fatal jewel, which Calisto has bought with the death of their predecessors (XIV, 128). The very words of the heroine (XX, 207, 213 ff.), the boasting of her mother (XVI, 157, 162), the apprehension (XII, 98; XVI, 156 ff., 162) and lamentation (XXI, 218, 223) of her father reveal the great care with which she has been raised, and show how the lives of all those surrounding her converge upon her. Thus, Melibea's portrait arises — apart from her own words and deeds — from an extremely delicate balance between the exaggerations of her lover, the cold remarks of the go-between, the admiration of the servants, the envy of the tarts, and the pride and anxiety of her parents.

ORGANIC UNITY AND CHANGE. Because each personage is a complete individual, his detailed portrayal is not a rigid composition, which would amount to a falsification of art and of life. Like Cervantes' characters — and like *homo sapiens* — those of *The Celestina* observe in their development a law of internal unity, a thoroughly clear line together with a no less clear freedom to vary it. At the same time, the variations permit one to recognize a coherent pattern. Calisto, passionate and verbose, consumed and destroyed by his love, has his moments of silence and of ennui (XIV, 130, 133, 137). Though weak and inactive, he is apt to show his resoluteness where his desire to satisfy his passion at any cost is at stake (XII, 88) and, though egoistic, he will recklessly rush to protect the servants he deems helpless (XIX, 198 ff.). These apparently discordant notes integrate his profile as a solitary dreamer in eternal maladjustment with reality. Celestina, whose mind is ever alert to her profit, can be seen working against her own interests when blinded by her addiction to wine (IV, 173 ff.), by jubilation over her professional triumph (V, 196 ff.), or by her very greed (XII, 104 ff.).

The characters change: this is evident with Melibea and with Pármeno, whose conduct swings from one extreme to the other before the reader's eyes, while neither *Pamphilus* nor even the *Book of Good Love* succeeded in using exclusively psychological methods to trace the heroine's complete emotional path from rejection to acceptance of love. But the other figures also oscillate, contradict one another, draw farther away from or closer to their original position. Sempronio, for example, realizes that Celestina will cheat him of his share in the spoils gained from Calisto; nevertheless, for a time he meekly prefers to deceive himself, and to believe that she will not dare to take advantage of him, until at last he can no longer help but admit the truth and, with pent-up hatred, he resorts to violence. Celestina enters the scene closely allied with Sempronio and hostile to Calisto. Very soon, through avarice and professional pride, she starts serving Calisto faithfully and divorces her interests from Sempronio's.

By an extraordinary innovation the characters not only vary within the work, each one changing according to his own law — that is, living — but also give the reader the feeling that they have already lived and changed. The characters have a history behind them. We know Celestina's with abundant detail: she has been the youngest of four daughters (IV, 172), a fact which subjectively increases the bitterness of her growing old. Once she was a beautiful (IV, 170 ff.), sought-after, arrogant courtesan (I, 69; VII, 253; IX, 41); later on, an amazingly prosperous and busy procuress (I, 59, 70 ff.; III, 132 f.; IX, 45 ff.). We know of her teacher (VII, 262) and of her deceased partner (III, 134 ff.; VII, 238 ff.; XII, 109) as well as of some unfortunate experiences with the law (II, 121; IV, 160; VII, 239, 242). We also learn a good deal about the past of Pármeno, son of Alberto and Claudina (I, 98 ff.), who as a child served Celestina (I, 69, 98) and then not a few other masters (XII, 96), until finally settling down at Calisto's house. Even Melibea has a past: the child-hood years in which Celestina knew her, when she had not yet "grown up and become a discreet and lovely young woman" (VI, 225), when her father, the more to enlighten her mind, made her read "ancient books" (XX, 213).

FLIGHT OF IMAGINATION. The presentation of these characters is so complete that it not only encompasses their factual reality, but also their daydreams. These occupy a good part of their lives, even in those most active and down-to-earth, such as Celestina, the servants and their lovers, and also in the most sedate, like Melibea's parents. On the other hand, not even Calisto wholly yields to a vague lyrical reverie. The characters of *The Celestina* duplicate their passionate living with a passionate and intense dreaming. They conceive of the circumstances they fear or yearn for as being tangibly present. The slightest impulse suffices for them to embark upon a minute portrayal of a person or a situation, themselves rising to a high pitch on hearing the piling-up of their own phrases. Calisto, for instance, breaks into rhetorical apostrophes the first time he meets Celestina, because he fails to see in her the actual reality — the hideous old hag in tattered clothes. He visualizes instead the coveted future and consequently addresses her thus (I, 90 f.) :

"Do you not see what a reverend person, what a dignity? . . . Oh virtuous old age, oh aged virtue! Oh glorious hope of my desired goal, o goal of my delightful hope! Oh salvation of my passion, defense against my torment, my regeneration, vivification of my life, resurrection from my death!"

Later, when Celestina reports to him the outcome of her first visit, the popular proverb she adduces ("Zamora wasn't won in a day") serves as a theme for Calisto's variations, which envisage his beloved as an impregnable city (VI, 221). Similarly, at the conclusion of the same act, Celestina's eulogy of Melibea, too parsimonious for his taste, ignites in him a fiery praise which not only passes in review Melibea's loveliness, but also that of all women past and present, their history and artifices to secure beauty, which he opposes to the naturalness of his lady and to her theological superiority (VI, 226 ff.). Calisto, skillful in the allegorical introspection of troubadouresque lyricism, addresses with concrete imagination his senses, his limbs (VI, 218 f., 222 f.), and Melibea's cord (VI, 220, 222). With the same *fougue,* without any further need of contact with reality, he later on "reconstructs" step by step the psychological process which was shaping up in the mind of the judge who has put to death his servants: he transforms their summary execution into a show of benevolence and muses on a life entirely devoted to his love (XIV, 137). However, it is not always possible to dissolve into words and dreams the harsh circumstances of the external world. On these occasions, when for example the lover's impatience clashes against cosmic order, Calisto grasps his only effective weapon (XIV, 139): "But you, sweet imagination, you who can, do help me."[3]

[3] A variation on a pious idiom underlining God's omnipotence; cf. Gonzalo de Berceo, *Milagros de Nuestra Señora* [Miracles of Our Lady], stanza 551 d; *Martirio de San Lorenzo* [Martyrdom of Saint Laurence], 45 d; *Sacrificio de la Misa* [Sacrifice of Mass], 47 c; the anonymous *Caballero Cifar,* ed. C. P. Wagner, Ann Arbor, 1929, p. 43; Alfonso Martínez de Toledo, *Arcipreste de Talavera,* ed. L. B. Simpson, Berkeley, 1939, pp. 85, 160. It would be difficult to bring out more adequately Calisto's dependence on his inner life, as well as his peculiar devoutness, than by his substituting in the old phrase "sweet imagination" for "God."

Melibea also inflames her passion by speaking. It is her own imagination which causes her to discover a sinful purpose behind the compliments paid to her by the young knight. In the interview with Celestina, at the earliest mention of Calisto's name, her excited imagination brings forth frightful punishments for the old woman (IV, 177 ff.). At the second, she mockingly recalls her melancholy suitor, pale and slender, and she takes pleasure in fathoming his thoughts (IV, 180). With equal intensity of imagination, but in an opposite sense, she appears in her soliloquy (X, 53) disconsolate at the thought of her delay, and fancying that because of a single day of disdainfulness, her surrender will no longer be appreciated. In an effort to stress the submission she owes to Calisto, her imagination wanders off to romantic extremes, so far removed from reality that their juvenile exaggeration lends an almost comical tinge to her impetuous outburst.[4] With comparable exaggeration, Melibea finally conjures up before her father a vision of grief for Calisto's death, a parade of dismal sounds, of mourning garments, of ruin and distraction, which first fill the city and then the entire world (XX, 211).

Celestina makes use of a practical imagination aimed at protecting her actions, and of a poetic fantasy capable of evoking the past or the future. The first especially marks her tactics, not coldly premeditated as those of Richard III or of Iago, but born (with typical Spanish improvisation), in the heat of the action, and adjusted to the varying circumstances in a masterly fashion. The latter breaks loose, even against her own interests, when certain traits of her character enter into play: her professional pride (III, 137), fear (IV, 153 ff.), love of wine (IV, 173; IX, 45 ff.). This poetic fantasy at times allies itself very subtly with the go-between's plans. Thus, the moving evocation of her lost youth (IV, 171) acts concomitantly as an epicurean inducement for Melibea, just as her lascivious memories infect the reluctant Areúsa (VII, 256) and the couples at her table (IX, 40 ff.), and as the lively portrayal of her time of glory serves to give the toothless old woman, with no more company than the jug, a prestige far superior to that of her seductive protégées (IX, 45 ff.).

[4] XVI, 159: "He may do with me and dispose of me at his pleasure. If it is his will to cross the sea, I shall go with him; if it is to circle the world, I wish he would take me along; if it is to sell me in enemies' land, I shall not refuse his desire." The last flight of fancy probably alludes to the "Niña de Gómez Arias," a maiden sold by her seducer to the Moors of Granada; her pathetic story inspired a popular song which, in turn, became the point of departure for a play by Luis Vélez de Guevara, later adapted by Calderón; see R. Rozzell, "The Song and Legend of Gómez Arias," *Hispanic Review,* XX (1952), 91-107.

The unworthy characters — Sempronio, Pármeno and Centurio — spur on their cowardice with their imagination. In Act I, Sempronio wonders which steps he should take, depicting for his own benefit the consequences of his intervention or of his inertia (I, 37 ff.). Once the enterprise is placed in Celestina's hands, fear of Pleberio's reprisals grips him (III, 140 ff.; XI, 75; XII, 85 ff.). His fear contaminates Pármeno who, as the more acute and sensitive of the two, becomes overjoyed as he imagines the rich share of the gains which will fall to him (XI, 72), and jumps with pleasure on enumerating the imaginary dangers from which he has extricated himself thanks to his lies (XII, 84 ff.). Out of sheer fright, Centurio fabricates pretexts for not carrying out the vengeance which Elicia and Areúsa have entrusted to him, and actualizes the reactions of both jades to each of his fibs (XVIII, 184). Furthermore, his delight in giving free course to his fantastic swagger is one of the notes which set him apart from the entire cast of *The Celestina*. Areúsa lives fearful of her neighbors' gossip, and of the punishment her soldier may inflict upon her (VII, 251 ff.). She particularizes the miseries of serving girls (IX, 42 ff.) in a spirited picture which had many imitators, Cervantes among others. Later, she eloquently bewails Celestina (XV, 145, 149), and lays poetic curses on Calisto and Melibea, exasperated above all because she imagines Melibea to be happy with Calisto's love and proud of the deaths which she has occasioned (XV, 149).[5]

OBSCENITY. The imaginative flight of the characters permits us to evaluate a strident note, by which *The Celestina* differs from most masterpieces of Spanish literature: the use of obscenity. Obscenity, scatological references, gluttony, idleness, and quarrels between people of low station provide an overdose of comical material in the Greco-Roman comedy and its offshoots, including the theater of the Modern Age. From the literary historian's viewpoint, the uniqueness of the *Tragicomedy* consists, once more, not in having retained one of the traditional elements, but in having discarded all the others.

What is the meaning of the three scenes and the few sayings in which obscenity appears in *The Celestina*? The undeniably spiritual quality of love in *The Celestina* — in harmony with the vivid imagination of the characters, and as a result of the influence of the *roman courtois* on its genesis — is in essence incompatible with obscenity,

[5] Owing to a confusion of which the "interpolator" (1502) seems to have grown aware too late (cf. XVII, 175), the names and some personal circumstances of Elicia and Areúsa have been interchanged in Acts XV, XVII, and XVIII; see *La originalidad artística de "La Celestina,"* Ch. XVII.

just as its austere technique, opposed to any extraneous tricks of the trade, cannot admit it as laughing matter. In *The Celestina* obscenity is a dramatic expedient, which adds depth to the outline of the characters and to the direct presentation of three decisive scenes. Sempronio is the moralist whose conduct belies his preaching. For this reason, although foolishly sentimental in all that concerns his own love, he is somewhat satirical and obscene judging Calisto's or Pármeno's (I, 44 ff.; VIII, 10 ff.). Pármeno, as an adolescent, is the one fondest of risqué quips (I, 66 ff.; 70 ff.; 79, 92, 97 ff.; VI, 205, 216). On returning from his adventure with Areúsa, he asserts his virility before the incredulous Sempronio with plain speech (VIII, 14). This is why Pármeno is the only person whom Celestina — perfectly aware of such juvenile foible — approaches with an indecorous joke (I, 95), which has the effect of immediately placing the two on an intimate footing. For her part, the old woman indulges in smutty witticisms as a senile compensation for the lust which she can no longer satisfy (III, 137 ff.; VII, 256 ff.; IX, 28, 41). In the faithful servants, the coarse comments with which they spice the lovemaking of their masters is mere envy, as Lucrecia's words concerning Calisto and Melibea make plain (XIX, 196).

The meaning of the three lewd scenes which the *Tragicomedy* enacts directly is no less clear. From Act I, Celestina tries to attract Pármeno, the most sagacious and recalcitrant of her opponents. In Act VII the skirmish continues without success. But what Celestina's dialectics and persuasion, Sempronio's example and Calisto's injustice have been unable to accomplish, the brutal impact of the senses achieves in an instant. The sight of Areúsa in bed breaks all Pármeno's intellectual and moral defenses, and this is the reason for its direct presentation. The scene marks a decisive step in the action, and sets off the characters of its three participants: the adolescent, dazzled by the erotic solicitation; the prostitute, vacillating and passive; and the old woman, aware of the weaknesses of both, steadily manœuvring them to her own advantage, and moreover enjoying herself in arousing the pleasure which she cannot share. As for the love scenes between the protagonists, since it is typical of the *Tragicomedy* to depict people in action — be it Celestina in the traffic of her house, or the servants at their chores — it was logical that it should not suppress the fulfillment of that love toward which the work is heading from its first page. Here too, the individuality of each person is sharply outlined. At the first rendezvous, Calisto initially shows himself eloquent, impatient and boastful of his triumph, then silent and sickened upon his collision with reality, from which he must draw away on the wings of his imagination in order to kindle again his love for Melibea. As for her, she successively falls prey to love, fear, bashfulness, regret for the error she has committed and, finally, she is all submission and eagerness to secure her lover's attachment. The groom Sosia is scornful and hard; the young page Tristán, sensually excited by envy of his master, quickly returns to his customary caution. In the last love scene, added in the 1502 edition, only Melibea's playful remonstrances and Lucrecia's spite suggest the amorous game; and throughout it there is no surfeit, no regret, but renewed tenderness. Unlike the previous scene, here the lovers' characters harmonize, as if reflecting a more mature phase of their passion. Their harmony, we know, ironically underlines the cruel death which awaits them. *The Celestina*, then, admits obscenity only as a dramatic resource, and handles it with unparalleled mastery, as far removed from Victorian prudishness as from the erotic obsession of our times.

ERUDITION. Erudition, common to most characters, although its censure is little less than obligatory in modern *Celestina* criticism, has not yet been examined in the light of its artistic function. It so happens that when *The Celestina* came to light, this kind of learning was infinitely less shocking than nowadays. In the first place, since Latin was the basis of all education, the apophthegms, anecdotes, and mythological motifs from Latin authors were incomparably better known than in our world, oriented toward practical and scientific learning, and toward national and modern languages. Apart from the decline of Greco-Roman studies since the eighteenth century, especially within the fabric of Hispanic culture, another, still more important factor contributes to the recoil of today's reader from the erudition in *The Celestina*. Until the close of the eighteenth century, Western man exalted human effort, reason, knowledge and, in art, craftsmanship, whereas ever since, there has predominated the cult of nature, emotion, the will, the subconscious, the biological and, in art, the cult of immediacy. Whence it follows that for the modern reader sincere expression of sentiments and such reminiscences as to him seem learned have become mutually incompatible, separated as they seemingly are by the abyss between life and literature.[6] But before Roman-

---

[6] Garcilaso de la Vega, *Eclogue I*, vv. 370 ff., on Doña Isabel Freyre's death in childbirth, clarifies, it would seem to me, this point. For most twentieth-century readers, imbued with the sacredness of maternity, Garcilaso's allusion to the Roman goddess Lucina and to the myth of Endymion may sound as bookish embellishments, petty and frivolous if measured against the biological dignity of such a death, and detracting from the warm tenderness

ticism, in a world willing to revere reason as the highest guide of human conduct in all fields, and which therefore respected knowledge and admired craftsmanship in art, reading was a vital experience; literature was neither opposed to nor artificially tacked on to life and, in consequence, learned reminiscences implied no sterility of thought, poverty of emotion, or lack of sincerity. Recall that, until the nineteenth century no critic branded *The Celestina* as pedantic; and that its Latin translator, Kaspar von Barth, as well as its English translator of the seventeenth century, James Mabbe, considerably increased the proportion of its mythological allusions.

Today's reader is further upset by the fact that not only is learning displayed by the characters in whom it may be admitted in strictly realistic terms (such as Calisto, Melibea, Pleberio), but also by Pármeno, Tristán, and especially by Celestina. Is this not a break in the artistic ideal of verisimilitude which has presided over the creation of the *Tragicomedy?* Clearly this is not the case. Benedetto Croce compared this apparent challenge to realism with the use of verse form in modern drama.[7] Indeed, erudition is but one aspect of the stylized language of all characters. It is an artificial and pleasing convention, analogous to that which bids all characters of the Spanish Golden Age theater speak in verse and all characters of an opera express themselves in song. The fact that Celestina and Pármeno adorn their words with classical reminiscences is no more unrealistic than the fact that all the impassioned characters of Rojas — or of Shakespeare for that matter — even in monologues, convey their meanings in superbly cadenced phrases, all linked by flawless argumentation. As Croce points out, the erudition of *The Celestina* (like its taste for picturesque enumeration and for folk-proverbs) is an aspect of its style, which at times — very felicitously — is concise, although in general amplification has been preferred.

With striking novelty, the authors of *The Celestina* enlisted this use of learned lore not only as stylistic material for the purpose of amplification, but also in the service of the drama and, above all, in character delineation. A cogent proof is the fact that the only two purely ornamental, not didactic, uses of mythology in the play are assigned to

of the passage. For Garcilaso, whose sincere attachment to Doña Isabel is well attested, those learned allusions must have been a means of bestowing artistic quality on a physiological condition almost grotesque, if one keeps in mind that in medieval and modern literature maternity was preponderantly a comical subject. See my study "Dido y su defensa en la literatura española," *Revista de Filología Hispánica,* IV (1942), 248 ff., and *La originalidad artística de "La Celestina,"* Ch. XIV, n. 13.

[7] *Poesia antica e moderna. Interpretazioni,* 3d ed., Bari, 1950, pp. 219 f.

Calisto, who is steeped in literature (VIII, 21 f.). Calisto says that he will not eat, "though Phoebus' horses be pastured first in those green meadows in which they are wont to graze when they have set an end to their journey." Sempronio, who has crammed his diatribe against women with quotations and authorities (I, 47 ff.), rejects Calisto's circumlocution: "Leave off, sir, these roundabout phrases, this poetizing. For that speech is not suitable which is not common to all, not shared by all, or which few understand. Say, 'though it be sunset' and all will know what you mean." But this rejection implies no such aversion to erudite circumlocution as is typical of today's reader, obsessed by his notion of immediacy. What it actually implies is the aversion of the pedant, stuffed with maxims and doctrinal matters, to the purely esthetic use of mythology. Like the apportioning of balladry to Sempronio and of courtly lyrics to Calisto, that of didactic and of ornamental allusion neatly profiles Sempronio's triviality against Calisto's refinement.[8]

PLEBERIO. For the balance of this chapter, let me deal in some detail with but one secondary character, Pleberio — a character so secondary that several imitations and adaptations of La Celestina have cut him out entirely (to their own disadvantage). Peculiar to Pleberio is his late appearance on the stage in Act XII, while he has been present from the outset in the thought of the other personages (I, 36), generally with a connotation of care and vigilance. This late appearance is all the more pathetic as Melibea's undoing has already been decided and also because, in conformity with the above noticed contrast between the archetype and its individual variation, Pleberio fails to exhibit himself as the overbearing master, surrounded by a staff of servants, and inflexibly upholding the honor of his family. Instead, he experiences an almost animal anxiety for the security of his daughter and wakes up at the slightest noise in her room. No less pathetic is the fact that Pleberio has total confidence in his daughter, and refuses to upbraid her or even to warn her. This very silence arouses in the young girl the painful awareness of the sorrow that she has in store for her parents.

Act XVI, added in the definitive version, forms a bridge between the concrete figure of the father, presented in Act XII, and the abstract figure, charged with the recitation of the concluding speech of the Tragicomedy. In Act XVI, a tragic parallel to the scene quoted

---

[8] The second instance of purely ornamental mythology occurs in Calisto's soliloquy (XIV, 138): "O resplendent Phoebus, hasten to enter on your wonted course!"

from Act XII, Pleberio shows his solicitude for the future of Melibea, whom he tenderly judges to be perfect, placing himself not on the biological plane of the previous episode, but on the social plane which Melibea is even then undercutting: thus functions the implacable irony which dominates the Act. Supported in his self-deceit by Alisa's maternal pride, Pleberio hesitates to exercise his authority despotically — which fact *a posteriori* would justify Melibea's guilt —, and he is inclined to grant her freedom to choose a husband, a situation allowing for the last chance of a happy ending. But, by a new ironic twist, he asks his wife's advice, and she draws him away from the truth which he was about to face. In this way Rojas carries the dramatic tension to the extreme, opposing Pleberio's apprehensive and reasonable temper to the blind obstinacy of his wife and daughter, and reinforcing the pessimistic vision of the world as a chaotic struggle. For the rationalistic optimism of Cervantes, Pleberio's sensible proposition would have guaranteed the natural order and, in consequence, the happiness of all parties.[9] In *The Celestina,* Pleberio's reason succumbs to the first attack of Alisa's impassioned error; and he even fails to come to a realization of the facts, let alone to avert the catastrophe.

Then, when Lucrecia summons him (XX, 203), alarmed by Melibea's uncontrollable sorrow at Calisto's death, the Pleberio of Act XII reappears, full of anxiety, eagerly going from his wife to his daughter, quick to satisfy all the caprices of his dear child and, at the same time, helplessly appealing to her compassion (XX, 203 ff.). Such an attitude causes surprise, as it is absolutely unusual in Spanish literature,[10] not only in works prior to or contemporary with Rojas, but even in our days, and it matches the no less exceptional intimacy between father and daughter. In a way, Rojas continues the humanistic comedy's focussing on the father-and-daughter relationship, while at the same time he discards its traditional pattern of harshness and rebellion persisting, for example, in *Romeo and Juliet.*

Pleberio's most extensive intervention occurs when he is called upon to pronounce the peroration (XXI, 216 ff.), like the "master" of the medieval representation — like the Doctor of *Everyman* — who, as the spectacle comes to a close, faces the public directly in order to

[9] See Américo Castro, *El pensamiento de Cervantes,* Madrid, 1925, pp. 129 ff.

[10] In all likelihood it is not by chance that in "The Captive's Story" (*Quixote,* Part I, Ch. xli), Cervantes chose a Moor, Agi Morato, for the only tragic embodiment of fatherly love in his entire *œuvre* (cf. *ibidem,* p. 147, Castro's, keen appraisal of this character's tragic quality), as if such an elemental feeling were ruled out for members of Western Christian society.

underscore the moral lesson. But, urged by his vital human sympathy, an essential aspect of his quality as a dramatist, Rojas keeps the didactic mask within the *Tragicomedy,* because that mask is at the same time a character, a concrete human case. And his lament, brimful of aphorisms and learned generalizing examples, ends on a note of heart-rending personal anguish. Between the remembrance of the past and the sadness of his anticipated loneliness, Pleberio sinks into ascetic meditation. His complaint: "How lonely I am!" (XXI, 221) shows him tortured by his imagination: the father visualizes himself in the future entering his daughter's chamber and finding it empty, calling her and waiting in vain for her response (XXI, 223).[11] Thanks to his gift for endowing each of his creatures with an individual history, Rojas reviews here all the experiences of the desolate father: the passions of youth, the ordered life of maturity, the toiling to ensure his daughter a wealthy inheritance (shortly before, XX, 213, she has mentioned his care in her upbringing), and the present catas-

[11] Pleberio's words ("What shall I do when I shall enter your chamber and find it solitary? What shall I do when you will not answer me if I call you? Who will be able to fill my great need of you?") sound as the theme of the beautiful Baroque variation in *King John,* III, 4: "Grief fills the room up of my absent child, Lies in his bed, walks up and down with me, Puts on his pretty looks, repeats his words, Remembers me of all his gracious parts, Stuffs out his vacant garments with his form." For a probable trace of *The Celestina,* I, 39 f., in *Twelfth Night,* cf. M. Carayon, "L'Amour et la Musique. Sur un passage de *La Celestina,*" *Revue de Littérature Comparée,* III (1923), 419-421. For the English translation (1506) and the three adaptations of the *Tragicomedy* available in Shakespeare's time, see J. H. Herriott's review (*RPh,* X [1957], 368) of L. B. Simpson's translation of the *Comedia.* Other coincidences, besides those well known, with *Romeo and Juliet* can be found, for example, in *Much Ado About Nothing,* III, 2: Benedick, in love with Beatrice, says to explain his sudden melancholy: "I have the toothache"; cf. *Celestina,* IV, 181. *The Winter's Tale,* I, 2: Leontes includes as a "note infallible" of being in love "wishing clocks more swift, Hours minutes; noon, midnight"; cf. *Celestina,* XIV, 138; IV, 3: Prince Florizel describes how his love for Perdita started: "I bless the time When my good falcon made her flight across Thy father's ground"; cf. *Celestina,* Argument to Act I. A number of coincidences might conceivably be explained on the ground of common belief and learning; significantly, though, they do not involve current topics; for example: *Love's Labors Lost,* II, 1: to praise his mistress, Boyet exclaims that Nature "did starve the general world beside, And prodigally gave them all to you"; cf. *Celestina,* VI, 226 f.; III, 1: the page Moth gives vent to his true feelings in an aside which, at Armado's bidding, he repeats, conveniently modified; cf. *Celestina,* I, 40 f., 45, 53 f., etc. *Much Ado About Nothing,* IV, 1: the Friar advises to spread the report that Hero is dead "for it so falls out That what we have we prize not to the worth, Whiles we enjoy it, but being lacked and lost, Why then we rack the value"; cf. *Celestina,* XIX, 201. I wonder whether, in the light of Calisto's and Doctor Faustus' tragic soliloquies before the clock, Touchstone's delightful meditation on his dial (*As You Like It,* II, 7) does not uncover a parodical purpose.

trophe. With the selfishness of a father and of an old man, Pleberio includes his daughter's destiny in his own, since he is unable to conceive of it save as the outcome of his own life. The enumeration of his endeavors, probably suggested by Petrarch's dialogue in *De remediis utriusque fortunae* [On the Remedies for Both Fortunes], I, 90, is a superb demonstration of how Rojas has dramatically recreated his prime sources. Petrarch's dialogue is a lengthy account of the provisions and labors after which the foolish man settles down to enjoy his prosperity, without heeding the brevity of life and the mutability of Fortune. Transcending these doctrinal platitudes, Rojas enumerates, in an evident effort of increasing their importance, only a few tasks, similar to, though not identical with, those of Petrarch. He does so not to accentuate the false security in which Pleberio was immersed, but to accentuate the dependence of his entire life on Melibea (XXI, 217 f.) :

"Oh this too hard father's heart! Why do you not break with grief, now that you are left without your beloved heiress? For whom did I raise towers? For whom did I acquire honors? For whom did I plant trees? For whom did I build ships?"

The subsequent words, in which Pleberio refuses to recognize Fortune's jurisdiction over life, depart completely from Petrarch — who specifically includes the loss of children among the blows of adverse Fortune — in order to stress the paternal love of Pleberio, who would willingly have redeemed his "plant in bloom" at the expense of his "large estate."

Pleberio's activities hardly befit a Castilian magnate, and on the other hand, he is not engaged in such typical occupations as the life of war and court. The reason for this incongruity seems to be that Rojas decided to divest the character of all environmental attributes,[12] tied to this or that region or caste, and to set him off, when he pronounces the concluding speech, as an example of human validity in general. Through this peculiar duality, there occurs in Pleberio, more than in any other figure, a blend of the individual condition with that which, by being elemental, is universal and goes beyond such literary

[12] A parallel case is the locale of the *Tragicomedy*, which has defied every precise geographic identification, because the authors have adroitly telescoped features of most cities, avoiding those traits which would give away a definite place (such as mentioning the name of its river, the presence of a University, or of the Court, a peculiar trade or industry, etc.). Similarly, though money and clothes play a prominent rôle, the authors use only the most general terms, thus preventing any inference about the time of the action that could otherwise be drawn from the prevailing currency or fashion. For a detailed discussion of this recoil from identifying details, see *La originalidad artística de "La Celestina,"* Ch. VI, end, and n. 10.

and social conventions as were in full vigor in Rojas' epoch and even much later. One cannot help being struck by the modernity (or, if you prefer a smaller measure of presumption, by the nonconventionality), the eternal and essential humanity of such a conception of the loving father, undone by the bereavement which leaves him lonesome in his old age, indignant with Fortune, World, and Love, who have all three taken his daughter from him, yet not uttering a single reproach against her. In this he shows the total understanding which she presupposed on opening her heart to him with unusual frankness.

Pleberio remains also silent on the loss of his honor and on the condemnation of her soul. Even more notable than in the youth Calisto, carried away by egoism and passion, is the absence of the Castilian sense of honor in the old father who, in this, defies literary tradition and contemporary reality. Equally surprising is — both here and at the beginning of Act XVI — the ascetic tone of his words, which are not at all devout, now and then intensified by the bitterest echoes of the Old Testament. Fernando de Rojas' status as a convert was bound to contribute to a creation so sharply divergent from all that Spanish literature offers. Artistically viewed, these two negative notes deeply accord with the elemental quality of a father with which Pleberio enters the stage in Act XII, and with the universal value of the lesson in disillusionment that closes the *Tragicomedy*.

I submit that a more profound and suggestive tracing of characters than one finds in *The Celestina* can hardly be imagined. At the same time, *The Celestina* is more than a study in characters; its straight action is basic and indissolubly amalgamated with the characters. This action ties together the twenty-one acts required for the unfolding of the detailed presentation of men and things. To be sure, some trivialities are all that occur in *The Celestina*, but they occur in this and in no other way because the personages, by dint of their unique characters, react to the external stimuli in this and in no other way: action and reaction are reciprocal and continuous as in the best drama, as in life itself.

Index

Abravanel, Isaac, 12
Aeneid, 24
Aetheria, 55
Agamemno, 68
Agi Morato, 95
Al margen de los clásicos, 22
Alberti, Leon Battista, 55
Alberto, 87
Alcaraz, 36
Alfonso VI, 75
Alfonso VIII, 75
Alfonso X the Learned, 6
Alfonso XI, 7
Alfonso de Cartagena, Bishop of
  Burgos, 11
Alisa, 59, 62 ff., 70, 73, 77, 82, 95
Allegory, 30 ff., 40
Amador de los Ríos, J., 12
Amar sin saber a quién, 68
America, 5, 12
Amor costante, L', 69
Amphitruo, 69
Andalusia, 7, 44
Andreas Capellanus, 31
Antes que todo es mi dama, 68
Apollonia, Saint, 60
Apuleius, 19
Arabic songs, 10, 20, 35, 47
Arabs, 6, 10 f., 20 f., 30 f., 36, 46 f.,
  50
Aragon, 11
Arcipreste de Talavera, 88
Areúsa, 51, 58, 61 f., 64, 69, 73, 80,
  82 f., 89 ff.
Ariosto, 52, 69
Aristotle, 66, 72
Art of Courtly Love, The, 31
Art of Love, 8, 23, 37
Arte nuevo de hacer comedias, 75
As You Like It, 96
Asensio, M. J., 71
Aside, 67, 68, 73, 96

Asinaria, 68
Augustine, Saint, 19 f.
Augustus, 24
Aulularia, 68
Autobiography in the *Book of Good
  Love,* 19 ff.
Avare, L', 68
Avignon, 2
Azorin, 22

Bacchides, 52, 68
Bâle, Council of, 11
Balzac, 19
Barth, Kaspar von, 85, 93
Baucis et Traso, 53
Baudelaire, 34
Beatrice (in Dante's *Vita Nuova*), 20
Beatrice (in Shakespeare's *Much
  Ado About Nothing*), 96
Beaumont and Fletcher, 69
Benedick, 96
Benedict XII, 49
benimerines, 7
Bergson, Henri, 83
Bible, 8, 22 f., 30 f., 98
Biscay, 7
Black Death, 7
Boccaccio, 16, 31
Bodmer, D., 47
Boethius, 19
Bonucci, A., 55
Book of Alexander, 18
Book of Delights, 21 ff., 27, 49
Book of Good Love: prose prologue,
  18, 25, 31, 34; stanza 1ab: 10;
  13cd: 25; 16 ff.: 35; 19bc: 2;
  44 ff.: 32; 70: 35; 76: 26; 78d:
  10; 105: 26; 115 ff.: 35 f.; 321 ff.:
  36 f.; 432 ff.: 27; 441d: 27;
  474 ff.: 8; 490 ff.: 37; 493ab: 2;
  653: 27, 38; 654 ff.: 39; 661c: 9;
  698: 69; 699 ff.: 27; 725 ff.: 40;

99